THE

BRIDE

OF

CHRIST

One Woman's Perspective

Linda, a true "Bride of Christ"

May the love of Christ deepen as well as your relationship w/ our Lord.

Thanks for your friendship, love and prayers.

Love,
Pat

THE
BRIDE
OF
CHRIST

One Woman's Perspective

PAT NOLAN

The Bride of Christ: One Woman's Perspective

ISBN 978-0-9788726-9-4

Published by HonorNet
PO Box 910
Sapulpa, OK 74067
www.honornet.net

CONTENTS

ACKNOWLEDGEMENTS

I WOULD LIKE TO THANK MY WONDERFUL and patient husband, Dan, whose love, strength, encouragement, prayers, and endless support helped me to emerge victorious over the circumstances that confronted us this past year. Thank you with all my heart, Dan.

Thanks to all my wonderful friends who encouraged me throughout this venture, continually praying for strength, wisdom, peace, and victory as God guided my heart and hand. (Yes, I also wrote this book longhand). How blessed we are to know you, Alleyne, Elloree, Lorraine L., Lorraine S., Shirley, Wilhelmina, Teresa, Martha, Cassie, Kathy, Holly, Deb, Susan, Donna, Linda, Carlton, Dana, Renee, Marie, Josie, Dolores, Eleanor,

Meg—my sister, Barb—and Dave, Ruth, Jim—Joanie, Dan, and all the others I have not mentioned. Please know that Dan and I so value your intercession, friendship, love, and prayers.

Much appreciation to Mary Ellen Breitwiser for encouraging me and praying for Dan and me throughout these very difficult months. And much appreciation for her editorial assistance.

INTRODUCTION

THE YEAR 2007 WAS VERY DIFFICULT for my husband and me. The past several months have taught me more than I expected about the compassion, love, faithfulness, and mercy of God as well as His utter sovereignty.

I knew that, as a Believer, I was a bride of Christ. However, I did not comprehend the magnitude of that position. As I experienced the strength and love of my husband, Dan, who surrounded and comforted me when my body was wracked with intense, nonstop, burning pain, I understood unconditional and sacrificial love as never before. I am so grateful to God for a husband who literally wished he could bear my pain. And thank God for close friends who expressed similar sentiments. I was truly overwhelmed and humbled.

I am blessed to have a husband and friends who have been there for me throughout this journey. One cannot put a price on such relationships. Even during my worst pain, when I genuinely thought I would not survive, they never let me give up. Truly this exemplifies the love of God expressed through His vessels.

My painful experience began the first part of July 2007 when I seriously injured my feet. I was in the yard with our English Setter puppy, Nava, when something caught her attention, and in a split second she lunged forward with all her might, pulling me along with her. Unfortunately, Nava stopped just as the arches of both my feet jammed against a giant, protruding tree root. Even though I was not barefoot, my feet were seriously injured.

Numerous trips to foot surgeons revealed only serious bruising to both arches of my feet. The surgeons believed that the burning pain I was experiencing was "normal" at that point, and said the healing process would take several months. Over the next seven or eight weeks, both feet seemed to show some improvement. Then—without warning—horrendous burning, stabbing pain began in my feet.

After being referred to another specialist, I endured a myriad of tests to rule out various diseases and conditions. Although, at times, it did not seem like God was with me during those seemingly endless dark days and nights of testing, the Lord never left me. He seemed so silent and distant from me at times, but He allowed me to experience His Peace and Presence when I had to undergo medical tests and procedures that scared me in the natural. When I surrendered to Him and His script, my Lord, my loving Husband, surrounded and protected me under the shadow of His wings. In those sterile, intimidating rooms filled with ominous-looking equipment, which sometimes made strange, loud, and repetitive noises, I could sense His Presence.

My first such experience involved an MRI of my brain. With my head secured in a helmet-like contraption and my body strapped down, I was required to remain absolutely still for 18 to 20 minutes, with a brief 10- to15-second break every now and then. The whole procedure took about an hour, and much of that time I was bombarded with endless clanging, banging, and jack-hammering noises.

During this entire procedure, my husband read to me from my first book, *The Cross of Christ: One Woman's Perspective*, only stopping when a brief break occurred. As Dan read the first 45 pages to me, his voice was so comforting to me, as were the words I had written as the Holy Spirit guided my heart and pen. As I gazed at my husband during the course of each test or procedure, I drew strength and peace from the love he extended to me.

All the test results came back negative, and during the process of deciding what to do next, my feet miraculously started to improve somewhat, even though the burning, stabbing pain continued to a lesser degree.

Our wonderful friends joined us in prayer, seeking God's wisdom and plan for my total healing. It was during our Christmas holiday—hours away from home—that God unveiled His divine plan and hand-picked surgeon.

In January 2008, during my first appointment, the surgeon identified the problems. On one foot, a lump of scar tissue, caused by a torn ligament, had formed near a nerve, causing constant pressure on the nerve. This condition required serious surgery during the first quarter of the year. Both feet had sustained severe bruising, particularly to the ligaments along the arches, and there was also a *conformation* issue—an abnormal anatomical structure of my feet that predisposed me to serious injury. This will also require surgical intervention in the near future. After all the years of hiking and walking, I had no clue of the existence of any such problems with my feet!

Now, nearly a year after sustaining the injuries, God knows exactly what the problems are and how they must be addressed now and down the road. My husband and I trust His loving hand to direct my surgeon as these issues are finally addressed. Although God directed us to this surgeon, we rest in the knowledge that He is our Healer and Miracle-working God, and that He will direct the surgeon's hands. He will never leave Dan and me nor forsake us as we place ourselves in His Hands and submit to His plan.

These past months, as God led us through this seemingly endless wilderness, have truly been difficult and painful. Like Job, who at times felt abandoned by God during his time of testing, I also felt abandoned by God and so alone. But He did not abandon or forsake me. During those darkest hours, when I did not feel I could face another day or night (24-7 of intense pain and sleep deprivation), the Holy Spirit kept wooing me to pick myself up by the bootstraps and face another day.

Through it all Dan and I felt our Lord enveloping us. It was as though He was holding us in His arms as a loving husband holds and comforts his bride. Thus, I began to comprehend even more the Believer's position as the bride of Christ. That relationship is the subject of this book.

In my first book I discussed the message of the Cross and how my relationship with God evolved from erroneous teaching that had me bound up in an exhausting faith struggle. Despite those erroneous beliefs, God's compassion reached down, and His loving Hand rescued me from death when I did not even know that I was at its very brink. Little did I know how this newfound freedom in the message of the Cross would impact *this* journey and lead me to a deeper understanding of that message as well as a new and deeper understanding of my position as a bride of Christ.

I also came through this year with greater understanding and experience of the compassion and love of God that heals and restores. I am healed and restored because of the Father's love shown to me through His Son.

Doctors who had been stymied by my condition rejoiced as they witnessed a miracle in progress. They were, and truly are, glad for me. One doctor even requested prayer for himself as he faced upcoming surgery. Another, who had declared that he does not believe in miracles, told us that when he confronts one before his eyes (like me), he does not discount it. Then he requested a copy of my first book and said he would read it because I had written it.

A dear and wise "mother in faith," Sister Fludd, told me all along that God would use this test to touch many people I never would have met otherwise. She was right. Of course, in the flesh, I wish I had not been given this assignment. But in God's sovereign will, He allowed it, including the unexpected surgical intervention that only He could have ordained. It is amazing to think about the material God uses and the paths He leads us down. Had we not returned to Lake Placid for

Christmas (we almost didn't go because of my intense pain), I would not have met the handpicked surgeon that God had chosen for me.

My miracle commenced just prior to our leaving town and weeks before any surgery had been scheduled. So doctors witnessed before their eyes an example of God's healing power. My turnaround was sudden and dramatic enough to grab their attention and override man's wisdom.

If you are presently facing a very difficult circumstance in your life, I pray that my words will inspire you to persevere instead of giving up. I pray that you, along with other readers, will discover a deeper understanding and experience of the love of a Husband for His bride. Come and read with me about Jesus, the Savior of the world, Who is a wonderful and loving Husband to His brides.

—*Pat Nolan*

CHAPTER 1

THE PINK ISLAND

MARCH 2, 2007—A DAY THAT MY husband and I will never forget. Nathan, our beloved English Setter, died that day, and I wondered, *How could this be?* He was so healthy and active, and he looked and acted much younger than his twelve years. Just the night before, Nathan had been prancing around, playing with his toys. Now he was gone. At a veterinary checkup that January, his doctors had marveled at his health and vigor.

We had a sense that something wasn't right shortly before his death. Even though he had been thoroughly checked out and there was no evidence of anything serious, I had a sense in my spirit that he was going to die. Oh, how we wanted more years with him! Nathan truly lived up to his name, "Gift of God." He was there for me when I almost died six years ago—and for the writing of my first book. In fact, I signed off on the back cover copy of my book on a Monday, and Friday afternoon he was gone.

My first book had been published, and I had received my copies the last week in March. How could all of this happen within these three-and-a-half weeks?

The twelve wonderful years God granted us to spend together passed all too quickly, but we thank God for the health, vigor, and sweetness this "special friend" displayed throughout his life.

Even though God prepared me for our separation about three days before his death, it was so hard to give Nathan back to Him. I remember sensing something foreboding. When I prayed, I sensed God telling me that Nathan's life was over and I needed to surrender him.

I lay in bed two or three nights before he died, crying my heart out before surrendering him to God (who owned him). Despite the wrenching pain and sadness, I had an overwhelming sense of God's Presence and

Peace as I surrendered Nathan and thanked God for giving him to us to enjoy for twelve years.

During the next two days, I sensed that Nathan knew too. There were little signs—the looks he gave me at times, his increased desire to be close to me, and his gaze that followed me as I prepared meals or sat down to work. He even climbed onto my lap more than usual. Yes, English Setters are known for their sweet, loveable personalities, and they will gladly sit on your lap, totally unaware of their size!

Grief, Shock, and Heart-wrenching Pain

It has been tough. The grieving process is still in progress, but God is faithful, loving, and so caring toward us, even as we grieve the loss of one of His four-legged creatures. Our Father has all things under His control, including the births and deaths of *all* our loved ones.

Through all the shock and heart-wrenching pain, we continue to know and experience the love and comfort of our compassionate and merciful God. He allowed Nathan to stay with us as I finished my first book. Later that week, he took his last breath. God sent the

Comforter to minister His Peace and Presence during those first days, and He continues to see us through.

NOTHING THAT HAPPENS IN YOUR LIFE IS INSIGNIFICANT TO GOD.

Again, we are getting more experience in His promises and His Word.

Weeping may endure for the night, but joy comes in the morning.

—Psalm 30:5

Nothing that happens in your life is insignificant to God. He cares about every detail of your life and mine, and He longs to share in our joys, sorrows, and grief. God loves you and me with such unconditional love. Why are we humans so slow to learn this? Why do we have such difficulty resting in and trusting the God who created us, promised to never leave or forsake us, and to meet our *every* need?

I can't even imagine the pain and sorrow the Father felt when He sent His Son to the Cross for us. Oh, what agony He must have suffered as He watched Jesus die. That is how much the God who created you loves you!

After our loss, Dan and I once again experienced the love, prayers, and caring of our true friends. It is as if we could feel them lifting us up in prayer. We treasured their phone calls to check up on us. We learn so much about God, ourselves, and our relationships at times like this.

While Nathan was alive, God used him in surprising and wonderful ways to touch many lives at an assisted living manor (for three years) and at a nursing home (for six months). It was amazing to watch how God used him to draw one of His lonely, hurting, or broken creatures out of the *prison* of his/her mind, if only for a short time. It was truly awe-inspiring to see the many smiles he generated and the many *re-awakenings* from withdrawal or a state of unawareness that took place because of Nathan's presence. Just to be an observer of how God used him in opening doors to minister the love and compassion of God to these precious people was a gift for my husband and me.

God never leaves or forsakes us. Not one of His creatures is ever forgotten. His mercy, grace, and faithfulness are new each morning. Praise Him.

> *This I recall to my mind, therefore have I hope. It is of the LORD's mercies that we are not consumed, because His compassions fail not. They are new every morning: great is Your faithfulness. The LORD is my portion, says my soul; therefore will I hope in Him.*
>
> —Lamentations 3:21-24

Nava

Although the sadness surrounding Nathan's death still surfaces at times, our home is no longer quiet. Eventually we brought home another precious gift— Nava, our three-and-a-half-month-old English Setter puppy. Nava (pronounced *Nah'vah*) is a Hebrew word that means "beautiful and pleasant." She is a handful! *Help!* What a shock to our life and routine to be confronted with "puppydom" once again.

THE PINK ISLAND

We did not enter into this new relationship without much prayer and waiting on God. We wanted His choice for us, and we wanted His timing. Throughout the process, God taught us even more about our stubborn, willful flesh. Oh, how we resist change; how we strive and struggle to force our own way. Yet, for the obedient heart that waits upon God, His will and script will be revealed.

I was so confident that God had another boy for us. After all, all of our dogs had been boys, and I assumed this would be His will for us again. Not so! It is interesting how God leads us to see our error and correct our faulty reasoning, if we are truly seeking His will.

A number of our friends were praying for us regarding a new creature to fill our home. They listened as I talked about waiting on God for our new puppy. One day, a friend prayed that God "would lead us to His four-legged creature for us." I picked up on that, wondering why God led Lorraine to pray that way. Hmm. I finally realized that I could be preventing God's best by excluding all female dogs. Did I wrestle with Him regarding this? Yes. But, as I surrendered my heart's desire and will to Him, I found myself willing to consider a girl—even eagerly desiring to see the one our beloved God would select for us.

It was about trusting the Lord and *not* leaning on *my* understanding—acknowledging Him in this way, too, and letting Him direct my path (decisions).

Things fall into place and are so much easier when we allow Proverbs 3:5-7 to rule in our hearts and lives:

> *Trust in the LORD with all your heart; and lean not unto your own understanding. In all your ways acknowledge Him, and He shall direct your paths. Be not wise in your own eyes: fear the LORD, and depart from evil.*
>
> —Proverbs 3:5-7

Nava is a sweetheart—a source of both joy and frustration. We have been thrust out of our comfort zones and our routines. It is amazing what God uses to prune and correct us. Oh, how He uses Nava to unveil flesh that needs to be dealt with. As you know, puppies develop our patience, especially as they test us to the limit. She will never replace Nathan, but we look forward to the life and relationship God has for us with her.

Before we could even look at puppies, God had to work some deep healing within our hearts. In my first book I expressed concern that my mother, a.k.a. "Hollywood" by her caring providers, would not live to see the completion of that book. She had undergone an unexpected arthroscopic surgery, and for some reason did not recover from the anesthesia. Wondering if she would live or die was, at first, a day-to-day experience, then week-to-week and month-to-month. Finally, after two-and-a-half months, it was apparent that she would live. As I write this chapter, "Hollywood" is still doing well. She received one of the first copies of *The Cross of Christ: One Woman's Perspective,* and she met Nava shortly after we brought her home.

Needless to say, after all we had been through, we needed some serious time away. We felt as if our hearts and heads had been in a vice grip. We were mentally, emotionally, and physically beat. Yet God had not failed nor abandoned us. To this day, His unfailing faithfulness surrounds us—even if we *feel* alone. So two-and-a-half weeks after Nathan died, we flew to God's place of renewing and refreshment for us.

Standing in "our" cliff above the pink sand beach and blue-green and emerald water, all care and anguish momentarily vanished as if carried out to sea by the flowing waves. God had removed us from all that had been raging around us and brought us to this beautiful island for healing, rest, and renewal.

As I gazed out across the sand to the multi-shaded water, I felt so light and free that time stood still. Once again our Father was allowing us to experience His gentle touch on our broken hearts and wearied minds.

These were truly times of renewing, refreshing, and strengthening by our God—our Father picking up His wounded children to heal the bruises and rekindle the flax (flame).

> *A bruised reed shall He not break, and the smoking flax shall He not quench: He shall bring forth judgment unto truth.*
>
> —Isaiah 42:3

We had come to Bermuda to allow God to help us rise from the ashes of grief and anguish.

Perhaps you have recently lost a loved one, and are dealing with a broken heart. Allow God to speak to your heart. He knows your pain. He knows what you are going through, and He is there to minister to you out of His heart of love and compassion.

Do you realize that not one sparrow falls to the ground without God taking notice? My Bible declares in Matthew 10:29-30 that it is true: "Are not two sparrows sold for a farthing? And one of them shall not fall on the ground without your Father. But the very hairs of your head are all numbered." He knows the pain, the loneliness, and the emptiness you have experienced.

Open your heart and let Him minister to you. He has come to rekindle the flame within your heart. He knows and comprehends the loss of a loved one—He gave His only begotten Son so you and I could spend eternity with Him. All of this is because of the Cross and our faith in Jesus Christ and His finished work at the Cross.

As I continued to stand on our cliff, gazing out at the water, a gentle breeze grazed my body. I could actually feel the Lord's Presence. It was as if His arms were holding me as a groom would hold his bride—

protecting, shielding, and comforting. We experienced such peace despite the sorrow that wrenched at our hearts.

Divine Provision

I marveled at the lovely accommodations our loving Lord had provided for us—the last suite—actually, the last available accommodation. The staff told us it was their best suite. I truly had not expected all this. It seemed so last minute, but God who knows the end from the beginning was prepared and knew exactly what we needed.

> *Declaring the end from the beginning, and from ancient times the things that are not yet done, saying, My counsel shall stand, and I will do all My pleasure:*
>
> —Isaiah 46:10

God, who knows all things, had arranged this trip well in advance of our needing it. He even arranged our schedules with all of those He had appointed to cross each other's paths and lives. I'll say more about that later.

It started to dawn on me that God was taking me further into the meaning and provisions of the Cross. He was taking me to my position as a bride of Jesus Christ.

As I gazed at the peace and beauty that surrounded me on beautiful Elbow Beach, I wondered what God's plan was for us and how it would unfold. Would we be able to enjoy His script despite the wrenching sadness that still surfaced when we least expected it? Could we really surrender our care and concern regarding "Hollywood"? And would we rest in His perfect plan? As I pondered these questions, I remembered the answer:

WE ARE TO CAST ALL OUR CARES UPON THE ONE WHO HAS ALL THINGS UNDER CONTROL.

Casting all your care upon Him; for He cares for you.

—1 Peter 5:7

We are exhorted to cast or throw all that has us worried and concerned or has caused us to be anxious and depressed—all our cares—once and for all upon the One who has all things under control. Furthermore, the literal translation of this verse tells us that *we* are *His concern*. Wow!

And in Matthew 6:27-34, we are instructed to avoid worry and anxiety! How can this be? Doesn't God need our help? Shouldn't we be spending time thinking of every possible scenario and then briefing God on how our issues or concerns should be resolved? Don't we need to worry, fret, and be anxious? What if God doesn't really have it covered?

Inevitably, the enemy will gladly lead us down the path of worst-case scenarios, with horrible outcomes, when we leave our position of faith in Jesus and what He accomplished for us at the Cross and revert to our flesh. It is so easy to do this, especially when situations and circumstances do not resolve quickly (or as we expected), or when tragic or other unpleasant events invade and touch our lives. These are the times that test our faith. Yet some of our most painful times provide the best opportunities for growth, and with them, the most opportunities for us to, once again, face the wickedness and strength of our fleshly nature.

I thought about our first trip to Bermuda four years earlier. God used that trip to provide more healing after my life-saving and unexpected heart surgery two years before, and He brought numerous people across our paths to whom I ministered and vice versa.

I wondered if this vacation would in any way resemble that trip. Honestly, I had not planned to do any ministering per se. After all, *we* were the fallen sparrows who needed our Father's gentle and compassionate arms lifting us up again.

Divine Appointments

I wondered if our paths would cross with any of the people who impacted our trip here four years prior. Hmmm. I recalled praying for, and with, every taxi driver who transported us around this beautiful island. During that trip, every one of our drivers was a man. Some of them big, burly men, and many or most were Believers. When they heard I was a minister, they wanted prayer—in their taxis! So I prayed for them, and then my husband paid them!

One day on that first trip, we had decided to trek up to another resort. After exploring Horseshoe Bay, we realized we were in the company of several hundred Believers who were attending their annual winter conference.

People from various islands and African nations as well as the U.S. descended upon Bermuda for their annual conference. One of the host pastors invited us to attend their Sunday service at the resort, and we did. One thing led to another, and before I knew it, I was on the platform, (in front of about 500 people, with television camera lights glaring) speaking about my ministry. What an unexpected and blessed experience! I will never forget it and neither will my husband. We were even guests at their banquet afterward. Oh, what fond memories.

What was God up to? I really didn't want to minister this time. I just wanted to rest, relax, and awaken from a deep sleep, during which God had removed all the hurt and anguish we still carried over from the U.S. That is *not* what happened.

As I acquainted myself with our accommodations and the changes that graced the resort, I sensed God prompting me to stop trying to figure it all out—to stop trying to convince Him that I knew better than He what I needed. These words from Proverbs came to my mind:

> *Trust in the LORD with all your heart; and lean not unto your own understanding. In all your ways acknowledge Him, and He shall direct your paths. Be not wise in your own eyes: fear the LORD, and depart from evil.*
>
> —Proverbs 3:5-7

IF YOU ARE A BELIEVER, YOU HAVE GOD'S ASSURANCE THAT HE IS WITH YOU IN EVERY SITUATION AND CIRCUMSTANCE YOU FACE.

"Be not wise in my own eyes." Hmmm. I must stop trying to figure it all out and look to Him—the One Who had won this battle for me at the Cross. I needed to allow Him to guide my heart and mind to the victory that He had already obtained for me regarding the issues at hand. I had to let Him unfold His plan that awaited my surrender at this beautiful venue. I was supposed to rest in the One Who promised to never fail or forsake us. Here I was at Hebrews 13:5 again!

If you are a Believer, you have God's assurance that He is with you in every situation and circumstance you face.

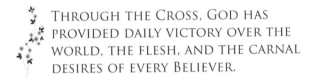

THROUGH THE CROSS, GOD HAS PROVIDED DAILY VICTORY OVER THE WORLD, THE FLESH, AND THE CARNAL DESIRES OF EVERY BELIEVER.

In my first book, I discussed at length the message of the Cross and its meaning for the Believer. All sin (for all mankind), past and future, was once and forever atoned for by our perfect Substitute, Jesus Christ. His precious Blood that was poured out upon the mercy seat ever speaks on the Believer's behalf. All we will ever need is found in the finished work of the Son. However, just as the Israelites received fresh manna daily from heaven (see Exodus 16), we Believers must position ourselves daily at the Cross and receive God's provision for our every need. Through the Cross, God has provided daily victory over the world, the flesh, and the carnal desires of every Believer. Jesus obtained the total victory for us 2000 years ago at the Cross.

Are you currently engulfed in sorrow, loss, pain, uncertainty, anxiety, depression, etc.? Do not give up. Do not despair. Do not succumb to the enemy's attempts to destroy you. Satan cannot do anything to a Believer without God knowing about it and allowing it. This horrible testing time has been permitted by your loving Father Who only has your best interests at heart. He will not permit Satan to go beyond the capacity of what you can bear. Truly. Do I always believe this? Deep down in my spirit, yes, I do believe it. But like you, I am but human, and I experience times when it seems as if God is not there—that the enemy is winning or will win.

GOD IS WAITING TO LIFT YOU UP AND MAKE WHOLE YOUR BROKEN OR WOUNDED HEART.

I believe these are the times when we will either permit God to prune us as He exposes yet more of our unruly, rebellious, and unredeemable flesh, or we will succumb to our own (or the enemy's) script and miss the victory God already has for us.

God is waiting to lift you up from the mire—to bind, heal, cure, and make whole your broken or wounded heart, all the while revealing more of His love for you and more of His character. His character is behind all that He has promised. Again, all this is possible because of the love He has for you. As you read this book, let God take you further into the depth of the sacrifice of His only begotten Son.

No sooner had we settled into our suite when members of the housekeeping staff began dropping by to introduce themselves. Our first acquaintance was Cynthia, who normally worked in another area of the resort. But for most of our stay, she was assigned to our location. Hmmm. What was this all about?

As we began to chat, we realized that we were all Christians who shared common interests and friends— friends we had met during our previous trip. Cynthia guided me to the new location of the local Christian bookstore. There I made the acquaintance of the new owner who happened to be good friends with the pastor who had invited us to that Sunday service four years earlier. Bermuda is a small island and, thus, many people know a lot of the same people, but this seemed much more than that! Sylvia, the bookstore owner, and I had a lot to share as women in ministry. I marveled at how God directed our paths, so that we women—children of God—could share about the Lord and at the same time encourage each other.

Although my book was being published at the time of our trip, I carried some promo book-cover fliers with me. Not only were all of the women I met very interested in my book (and wanted copies), but they were also very encouraging and supportive. It became apparent that the message of the Cross was being neglected in favor of man's programs that so subtly brought man back under the Law. And the women I met were adamant regarding our salvation being through Jesus Christ and the Cross. Period! Wow! Even Bermudian Christians were being challenged by good programs that only served to subtly bind man, once again, to legalism and self-efforts.

Why was this spiritual adultery so pervasive? And why did it continue to go seemingly unnoticed in much of the Church? Did God unveil our eyes because of the sincere cries of our hearts to know Him (and ourselves, our hindering flesh) more and more? Is it because we desire to have our fig leaves exposed for what they really are?

Sharing about our faith, our families, and our lives really helped us relax and bask in the rest and refreshment our loving Father had provided for us. It did not take long for word to get out that a Christian author and her Christian husband were at Sea Grape. It was time for God's next divine appointment.

Sandra, the head of housekeeping for our area, came to make her acquaintance. After chatting for a few moments, it became quite obvious that God had truly ordained this meeting. Not only did she want me to lay hands on her head and pray, but she also wanted to talk about the ministry she once had. Someone (with authority) in her church had told her she could no longer minister because she worked on Sundays! She so wanted to please God and fulfill her call, but her good job required working Sundays, and she had to provide for her family!

God used this opportunity to draw me out of my shell so I could minister to her. The lie—the oppression that had caused all the woman's problems—broke, and this child of God left a new woman on fire for God. Interestingly enough, she started ministering to the people God brought across her path that very evening. Sandra continues to minister to fellow employees seeking counsel and prayer—all without compromising the time owed their employer.

Before she left our room that day, I asked her to pray for me. God truly wanted this for both of us. I shared the story of my mother and Nathan with her, and she sensed my pain and need for healing. I never cease to be amazed when I think that this was the script God had ordained to advance His will in both of our lives. Why? Because He loves both Sandra and me that much!

A day or two later she returned to share the assignments God had placed in her path. It was wonderful to witness the joy in Sandra's heart and the fresh excitement. God used two of His children to minister to each other—even two "wounded sparrows" still have the capacity to minister the love of God. The result was a new resolve to minister to others. All we had to do was be willing to heed His call and go where and when He sent us.

God never promised us a life without sorrow, grief, or pain, but He did promise to never leave us nor forsake us and to provide whatever is necessary to be victorious in each and every situation. Again, everything we need has been provided for through Jesus and the finished work of the Cross.

> *There has no temptation taken you but such as is common to man: but God is faithful, who will not suffer you to be tempted above that you are able; but will with the temptation also make a way to escape, that you may be able to bear it.*
> —1 Corinthians 10:13

 GOD ALREADY KNOWS ABOUT EVERY SITUATION OR CIRCUMSTANCE YOU WILL EVER FACE.

We have God's assurance that He does not permit anything in our lives that cannot be victoriously overcome by faith in Jesus and the Cross. He knows each of our failings and frailties, but as we fix our eyes on Jesus and the Cross, God will reveal the way of escape, the way of victory He uniquely designed for us.

As we surrender to Him, putting our trust in Him, He will bring us out of or see us through any trying situation. Even if the circumstances you are facing have not yet changed in the natural, please believe me when I say that God is working on it. Think about this. God already knows about every situation or circumstance you will ever face. Although in Christ, you and I have already been delivered from the power of every struggle, the struggle has the potential to harm, overwhelm, captivate, or destroy us. But by looking to and depending on Christ in faith—and the fact that He alone defeated every enemy and won the victory regarding every battle we will ever face—you and I can walk out unscathed by the enemy's script and glorify God instead.

Believers are meant to be victorious. Jesus overcame the world, the flesh, and the devil for us. That is how much we are loved!

Remember Job in the Old Testament book of the same name? Satan had to obtain permission from God to do the things he did to Job and his family. This is also true for you, Believer. Absolutely nothing happens in your life without God knowing it or allowing it. Why did God allow Satan to do what he did to Job? I believe it is because He knew that Job would ultimately win. God knew that Job would not forsake Him, his God.

God—the Source of Victory

Consider Daniel, another Old Testament hero from the book of the same name, and his three friends, Shadrach, Meshach, and Abed-nego. Perhaps you have heard of Daniel's miraculous deliverance from the lion's den (Daniel 6) or his three friends' miraculous deliverance from the fiery furnace (Daniel 3). In each circumstance God only permitted Satan (via evil kings) to go so far. He delivered His people from that which was intended to kill them. Oh, the unfailing faithfulness of God.

Let us briefly examine Shadrach, Meshach and Abed-nego's ordeal in the fiery furnace. These three men had refused to obey evil king Nebuchadnezzar's decrees to worship (as their god) the golden image that he had erected. Their faith remained steadfast in the one true God, and despite any consequences they refused to forsake Him. King Nebuchadnezzar threatened to cast them into the midst of a fiery furnace if they refused to bow down and worship his graven image. Further, he promised that their fate would be timed for the very moment of their refusal:

> *…but if you worship not, you shall be cast the same hour into the midst of a burning fiery furnace; and who is that God who shall deliver you out of my hands?*
>
> —Daniel 3:15b

Oh, the arrogance and pride of that wicked king!

In verse 17 of this same chapter, the three men told the king that the God whom they served was able to deliver them out of the furnace as well as his hand. Their response obviously incensed Nebuchadnezzar, who demanded they be cast into a furnace that was seven times hotter than usual. It is known that the Babylonians recognized seven planets and had a god for each planet. So this could be the reason why Nebuchadnezzar ordered the furnace to be seven times hotter than usual—to appease his seven gods.

After the three men were bound in all their garments (verse 21), they were cast into the fire. Perhaps the king wanted to hasten their deaths, as their clothing most certainly was flammable. Also, being bound up as such, the men could not attempt to escape.

As you may know, things did not go as Nebuchadnezzar anticipated. Verses 24 through 28 relate what transpired:

> Then Nebuchadnezzar the king was astonied, and rose up in haste, and spoke, and said unto his counselors, Did not we cast three men bound into the midst of the fire? They answered and said unto the king, True, O king. He answered and said, Lo, I see four men loose, walking in the midst of the fire, and they have no hurt; and the form of the fourth is like the Son of God. Then Nebuchadnezzar came near to the mouth of the burning fiery furnace, and spoke and said, Shadrach, Meshach, and Abed-nego, you servants of the Most High God, come forth, and come hither. Then Shadrach, Meshach, and Abed-nego, came forth of the midst of the fire. And the princes, governors, and captains, and the

king's counselors, being gathered together, saw these men, upon whose bodies the fire had no power, nor was an hair of their head singed, neither were their coats changed, nor the smell of fire had passed on them. Then Nebuchadnezzar spoke, and said, Blessed be the God of Shadrach, Meshach, and Abed-nego, Who has sent his Angel, and delivered His servants who trusted in Him, and have changed the king's word, and yielded their bodies, that they might not serve nor worship any god, except their own God.

—Daniel 3:24-28

Not only did the king and his men see the three men walking around in that fiery furnace, but a fourth man was also in there walking around with them. None of the men were harmed or burned, and King Nebuchadnezzar himself declared that "the form of the fourth is like the Son of God" (vs. 25). When the three men were summoned from the fire and examined, not a hair or any part of their bodies or clothing were burned or singed, and neither did they smell of fire! In the face of this evidence, the king acknowledged the supremacy of the Hebrew's God, Jehovah, over all his (false) gods.

Note that God did not *deliver* His three servants *from* having to go through the trial, but He most assuredly *delivered* them *through* it.

Jesus, our sacrificing Peace, is there with us in every trial to be our Peace and our Source of victory—either delivering us out of the trial or in it. We have God's promises:

> *Let your conversation be without covetousness; and be content with such things as you have: for He has said, I will never leave you, nor forsake you.*

> —Hebrews 13:5

The literal translation says that the Lord Himself personally made this promise. In verse 6, we have the Lord's promise that no one can do more to us than the Lord Himself permits!

…The Lord is my helper, and I will not fear what man shall do unto me.

—Hebrews 13:6

ALL THE HURTS OF LIFE WERE DEALT WITH, ONCE AND FOR ALL, AT THE CROSS.

If you are weary, tired, broken, wounded, or hurt, be assured that the Lord hears your cries and sees your tears. Luke 4:18 tells us that Jesus came to heal the brokenhearted as well as to set at liberty those who have been bruised. Our broken hearts are buried, i.e., healed, cured, and made whole, through our faith in Jesus and His finished work at the Cross. Likewise, all the hurts or vicissitudes of life that have bound us in mental, emotional, or spiritual prisons were dealt with, once and for all, at the Cross. It is the Holy Spirit's job to affect these truths in our hearts and lives. Let Him. Cry out to Jesus, who understands and bore your pain, and let Him heal you. He wants you to be unburied, unfettered, and free. He went to the Cross for you and me. God is our Peace. To God alone be the glory forever.

I am so glad we went to Bermuda last winter. Our new friends look forward to our return next year, and so do we. It will be neat to see how God advances His script in all our lives, including increasing our understanding of being married to His Son—brides of Christ.

Even as I wrote this chapter, His loving arms held me as a loving husband would hold his precious bride.

CHAPTER 2

THE HILLS AND FIELDS

HIGH UP IN THE HILLS, I FEEL A world away from life with all its complexities. It is so peaceful, especially on those days when a soft, gentle breeze envelops my body. I look around at God's beautiful creation, and I'm very grateful that I can come here and get rest and renewal, all while enjoying my horse.

I cannot believe that "Red" and I have been together for twenty-one years. His registered name is *Rajah Fleet*, but he was very appropriately named Red due to his color. I had my first riding lesson on Red twenty-one summers ago, and we have been together ever since. Although he is 28 years old, to look at him and watch him, one would never suspect it. I truly thank God for preserving him all these years and giving us a special bond and relationship that is so unique to us.

How many times he has carried me up and down hills, through fields and woods, be it for a cross-country ride or just for fun. So many times I have come to the barn, needing to relax and just rest in God's Presence, and Red faithfully helped to fulfill this need.

How many times I have come to the barn with some pressing issue only to find it lifted from my heart and mind. It is at times like these that I find I have truly cast my cares and concerns upon the Lord and am free to hear from Him and enjoy His Peace. Many times I have noticed that little pains from overstretching and overuse disappear when I mount Red and we set off on God's "course."

So many times the stable owner and my instructor, Cassie, and I have traversed the hills and fields on our trusty mounts and found peace and release. And many times, while riding, I have been blessed with ideas or needed answers to questions I have had. When my husband's trusty mount, Poncho, was still living, Dan often received knowledge of witty inventions or solutions to research problems while riding. It is so amazing who and what God uses in directing our hearts and lives to cease from self-effort and to trust and rest in Him. God already has everything all figured out—we just need to let go of all that binds or confounds our hearts and minds and wait upon the One Who knows all things.

Free—but Still Under the Law?

God has all the answers, and when He reveals His marching orders to us, we must be obedient and walk them out. Easier said than done, huh? Oh, how our flesh argues and rebels. I realize more and more that our loving God allows these frustrating times to make us more aware of the sin nature that ever seeks to be god in our lives—and to reaffirm that our only salvation from it is through Jesus Christ and His finished work at the Cross.

Have you ever wondered why victory in certain areas of your life seems to elude you? Do you feel as if you are the only one who experiences this? Not so. All of us have weaknesses and issues that are not so easily overcome. The enemy wants us to believe that we are the exception—that God is displeased with us or that we must remain that way for the rest of our earthly lives, but that is a lie.

Believe me, you are not the only one to hear and receive the message of the Cross only to find yourself engaged in some seemingly hopeless battle. Why can't we accept the fact that Jesus' sacrifice at the Cross settled that issue 2000 years ago? We believe and see the evidence in some areas of our lives, yet we seem to be blinded in others. Paul said:

> *[God] having forgiven you all trespasses; blotting out the handwriting of Ordinances that was against us, which was contrary to us, and took it out of the way, nailing it to His Cross; and having spoiled principalities and powers, He made a show of them openly, triumphing over them in it.*
> —Colossians 2:13-15

We seem to forget that we are no longer subject to the old Law, and Paul had the same problem. He knew he was married to Christ—as a Believer, that is—but he sometimes felt and acted like a spiritual adulterer.

Know ye not, Brethren, (for I speak to them who know the Law;) how that the Law has dominion over a man as long as he lives? For the woman which has an husband is bound by the Law to her husband so long as he lives; but if the husband be dead, she is loosed from the Law of her husband. So then if, while her husband lives, she be married to another man, she shall be called an adulteress: but if her husband be dead, she is free from that Law; so that she is no adulteress, though she be married to another man. Wherefore, my Brethren, you also are become dead to the Law by the body of Christ; that you should be married to another, even to Him Who is raised from the dead, that we should bring forth fruit unto God. For when we were in the flesh, the motions of sins, which were by the Law, did work in our members to bring forth fruit unto death. But now we are delivered from the Law, that being dead wherein we were held; that we should serve in newness of Spirit, and

not in the oldness of the letter. What shall we say then? Is the Law sin? God forbid. No, I had not known sin, but by the Law: for I had not known lust, except the Law had said, You shall not covet.
—Romans 7:1-7

WE MUST CONTINUALLY PLACE OUR FAITH IN JESUS AND HIS FINISHED WORK AT THE CROSS IN ORDER TO EXPERIENCE THE VICTORY HE WON FOR US.

In these seven verses, Paul discusses the Law and sin. When we become Believers, we are delivered from the Law and put under the realm of God's grace.

For sin shall not have dominion over you: for you are not under the Law, but under Grace.
—Romans 6:14

As Believers, we must continually place our faith in Jesus and His finished work at the Cross in order to experience the victory He won for us, once and for all, over the world, the flesh, and the devil. Any reversion to self-effort will take us out of this realm of grace and place us back under the Law.

In the first four verses of Romans 7, Paul uses the analogy of a marriage bond to illustrate the dilemma many of us Believers find ourselves in.

When we became a bride of Christ, we became married to Christ. This was not our doing. It was in God's plan of salvation that we were baptized in Christ's death, thus, died with Him (positionally), were buried with Him, and rose with Him to newness of life, all via the work of the Holy Spirit within us. We are no longer in Adam, but in Jesus Christ. We are no longer under the Law or bound to the Law. We are in God's realm of grace as a bride of Christ.

Jesus perfectly fulfilled the Law, not for Himself but in order that we could be married to Him and experience all the benefits that His perfect sacrifice at Calvary provided for us. He did it all for you and me. Wow! That is why Paul writes in the last part of verse 4 "that we should bring forth fruit unto God."

In verse 5 we learn that the purpose of the Law was to reveal to man his sinful, wicked nature. Otherwise, man would not know he had need of a Redeemer. Verses 6 and 7 again remind the Believer that the Law was once and forever fulfilled by Christ who paid the full penalty for each one of us so that we, as His bride, are now free to serve Him in newness of Spirit. It is the Holy Spirit's job to affect in us the finished work of the Son through the victory He obtained for us. However, this only comes as we continually place our faith in Jesus and what He did for us at the Cross.

But, alas, it is not so easy! Why do so many of us still struggle against a specific sin or addiction? Paul provides answers in the remaining verses of chapter 7. However, before I discuss them, there are a few other issues that need to be settled.

Look at Romans 8:1-2:

> *There is therefore now no condemnation to them which are in Christ Jesus, who walk not after the flesh, but after the Spirit. For the Law of the Spirit of Life in Christ Jesus has made me free from the Law of sin and death.*

No Condemnation

God specifically tells us that there is absolutely no condemnation (or condemning sentence of guilt) to Believers. How can this be? Shouldn't people feel condemned for repeated failures or their inability to overcome specific sins, habits, or addictions after becoming Believers? And especially if they have been Believers for "forty years and know better"? No! No! No! God does not condemn us for our repeated failures or weaknesses.

All our failures and weaknesses were atoned for at Calvary by His Son. Jesus alone atoned for every one of our sins FOREVER, winning every victory we will ever need. It is the Holy Spirit's job to make this truth real or experiential in the lives of Believers. However, Believers cannot fulfill their ministries if they are consciously or unconsciously depending on their own strength in warring against lingering sins, habits, mindsets, or addictions, while thinking how displeased God is because they are still failing.

Boy, this can wreak havoc with one's mind and emotions. Some Believers convince themselves that they must try harder, pray more, study the Bible more, attend more church services (all good in the proper perspective), but when they only do this because they think God expects it of them, the result will be continued failure and bondage. Why? Because unknowingly, or due to ignorance of the message of the Cross, such Believers place themselves back under legalism, back under the Law.

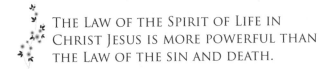

THE LAW OF THE SPIRIT OF LIFE IN CHRIST JESUS IS MORE POWERFUL THAN THE LAW OF THE SIN AND DEATH.

Remember, Jesus perfectly fulfilled all that the Law demanded and set Believers free to serve one another and the Lord Jesus Christ. We cannot serve God and man at the same time but, oh, how we try at times. Our flesh is slow to die. In verse 2, we are reminded that "the Law of the Spirit of Life in Christ Jesus" (faith in what Jesus accomplished for us at Calvary) is more powerful than the Law of sin and death.

I believe the original text says: "The Law of the sins and death." Hmmm. The Law of the Spirit of Life in Christ Jesus is more powerful than the Law of the sin and death. Everything that you have been fighting against in your own strength or ability has already been dealt with and defeated for you at Calvary.

Thus, no matter how often or how deeply you sin as a Believer, you are not under condemnation or a condemning sentence of guilt any more. And you should not place yourself under condemnation or guilt. No matter how vile the sin or the severity or duration of the habit or addiction, God is not condemning you (the Believer). Neither should you condemn yourself. Doing so would just keep you in bondage to guilt, shame, and hopelessness.

The enemy loves it when Believers remain on this hopeless path. When people operate under legalism, they remove themselves from grace. And, positionally, all Believers are now in the realm of God's grace. Many, though, are not experiencing this position of grace in their daily lives. Again, it is only ignorance regarding the fullness of salvation that was provided for us through the finished work of the Son at the Cross that keeps man in bondage.

Free Indeed!
Remember, we Believers are finished with the Law and are now married to another. His name is Jesus Christ. We are His Bride. To be married to Christ and, at the

same time, attempt to serve or please God via our own efforts or merits places us back under the Law. Once again, we often unknowingly engage in "spiritual adultery."

Please realize that I am not advocating a license to sin. I am telling all who have fought so hard in their own misguided strength or efforts that you and I are FREE. We are really FREE, despite any daily experience that says otherwise. The following verses support this truth:

> *If the Son therefore shall make you free, you shall be free indeed.*
>
> —John 8:36

GOD TRULY PROVIDED FREEDOM FOR EVERY ONE OF OUR LINGERING SINS, HABITS, ADDICTIONS, AND BONDAGES.

> *Knowing this, that our old man is crucified with Him, that the body of sin might be destroyed, that henceforth we should not serve sin.*
>
> —Romans 6:6

The phrase, "that the body of sin might be destroyed" means that the power of sin is broken. God truly provided freedom for every one of our lingering sins, habits, addictions, and bondages. A death blow was struck to the roots of them at the Cross. In God's mind, Believers are now positionally free. How He longs for this to be our daily experience.

Too often our efforts to overcome sin interfere with the Holy Spirit's job. But God will not share His glory. By not accepting the gift of freedom, we impede the Holy Spirit's work. But God is so patient with His stubborn and ignorant children. He never gives up on us.

Another rendering of Romans 6:6 lies in knowing this: that our old man is crucified with Him that the body of sin might be "loosed." In other words, the sins or bondages that have held us captive have been brought to naught or done away with—again, due to Jesus' finished work at Calvary for you and me.

And in line with Romans 7, another way of looking at this is that our former marriage to the Law (and, thus, to the Law of sin and death) has been rendered null and void because we are now married to another. We are Christ's brides.

GOD ACCEPTS YOU AND ME AS WE ARE
AND WHERE WE ARE RIGHT NOW.

If we continue to struggle as Paul did, then we who are married to Christ remain "married" to, or in bondage to, our former husband—the Law. Now do you have a better understanding of the spiritual adultery that has been so subtly operating in our hearts and lives? Remember, *it is not sinless perfection, but freedom from sinful dominion.* We do not arrive at this revelation overnight, and we most certainly do not experience this truth overnight. We grow in the grace and knowledge of our Lord and Savior, Jesus Christ.

God accepts you and me as we are and where we are right now. The Bible provides further hope and encouragement.

> *But now we are delivered from the Law, that being dead wherein we were held; that we should serve in newness of Spirit, and not in the oldness of the letter.*
>
> —Romans 7:6

Paul is telling Believers that they are meant to serve God "in newness of Spirit," in total dependence upon the finished work by the Son. We were brought back from the hands of Satan. We no longer belong to him and neither do our lives. The salvation God provided for us is complete. Yet we still struggle. Do not give up. Consider these words:

What shall we say then? Is the Law sin? God forbid. No, I had not known sin, but by the Law: for I had not known lust, except the Law had said, You shall not covet. But sin, taking occasion by the Commandment, wrought in me all manner of concupiscence. For without the Law sin was dead. For I was alive without the Law once: but when the Commandment came, sin revived, and I died. And the Commandment, which was ordained to life, I found to be unto death. For sin, taking occasion by the Commandment, deceived me, and by it slew me.

—Romans 7:7-11

BY FOLLOWING GOD'S PLAN, BELIEVERS BRING FORTH THE FRUIT OF THE SPIRIT.

The New Covenant

I want you to realize that Paul personally agonized with the dilemma of spiritual adultery. Remember, the Law of Moses was given to reveal man's sinfulness. The Law of Moses explicitly defined sin, but gave no power in itself to overcome sin. Moses carried God's Law down from the mount to God's people. The two tablets of stone God gave to Moses were part of the Old Covenant. Believers today are under the New Covenant, in which God places His laws in our hearts and minds through faith in Jesus. So the Law finds its fulfillment in those of us who place our faith exclusively in Jesus Christ and what He did for us at the Cross— not in man's efforts, determination, or programs. And by following God's plan, Believers bring forth the fruit of the Spirit because the Holy Spirit will be able to fulfill His mission in our hearts and lives, enabling us to walk after the Spirit and, thus, exhibit the fruit of the Spirit.

That the Righteousness of the Law might be fulfilled in us, who walk not after the flesh, but after the Spirit.

—Romans 8:4

In 2 Corinthians 3, we are shown that the Law of Moses does not even begin to compare with the glory of the New Covenant. In verse 9, Paul reminds us that the Cross permits great and wonderful victories to be wrought in our lives—again, provided that our faith is exclusively in the Cross and not some mixed message that attempts to live by grace utilizing some aspects of the Law.

For if the ministration of condemnation be glory, much more does the ministration of Righteousness exceed in glory.

—2 Corinthians 3:9

Remember the Pharisees, scribes, and doctors of the Law? They spent their lives debating the true meaning of the Law, attempting to achieve perfection in their own efforts and proudly displaying their self-righteousness. In the book of Matthew, Jesus spoke of His coming to fulfill the Law of Moses. In His death, burial, and resurrection, the New Covenant was ushered in. He was revealing the standing of all righteousness, and the absolute necessity of the New Birth.

> *Think not that I am come to destroy the Law, or the Prophets: I am not come to destroy, but to fulfill. For verily I say unto you, Till Heaven and Earth pass, one jot or one tittle shall in no wise pass from the Law, till all be fulfilled. Whosoever therefore shall break one of these least Commandments, and shall teach men so, he shall be called the least in the Kingdom of Heaven: but whosoever shall do and teach them, the same shall be called great in the Kingdom of Heaven. For I say unto you, That except your righteousness shall exceed the righteousness of the Scribes and Pharisees, you shall in no case enter into the Kingdom of Heaven.*
> —Matthew 5:17-20

Yet to this day, unsaved man denies his need for a Savior, and the legalistic Christian continues to serve

God in the oldness of the letter rather than the newness of the Spirit.

God looks at the heart. Flesh forever seeks to somehow earn God's favor, covering his sinfulness with ever-changing fig leaves. This is the dilemma Paul speaks of in Romans 7. In fact, he even expounds on this in his letter to the Philippians in chapter 3.

> *Circumcised the eighth day, of the stock of Israel, of the Tribe of Benjamin, an Hebrew of the Hebrews; as touching the Law, a Pharisee; concerning zeal, persecuting the Church; touching the Righteousness which is in the Law, blameless. But what things were gain to me, those I counted loss for Christ. Yea doubtless, and I count all things but loss for the excellency of the knowledge of Christ Jesus my Lord: for Whom I have suffered the loss of all things, and do count them but dung, that I may win Christ, and be found in Him, not having mine own Righteousness, which is of the Law, but that which is through the Faith of Christ, the Righteousness which is of God by faith: That I may know Him, and the power of*

His Resurrection, and the fellowship of His sufferings, being made conformable unto His death; if by any means I might attain unto the Resurrection of the dead. Not as though I had already attained, either were already perfect: but I follow after, if that I may apprehend that for which also I am apprehended of Christ Jesus. Brethren, I count not myself to have apprehended: but this one thing I do, forgetting those things which are behind, reaching forth unto those things which are before, I press toward the mark for the prize of the high calling of God in Christ Jesus.

—Philippians 3:5-14

Righteousness by Faith

Paul reminds the Philippians of his Jewish background, with his lineage going back to Abraham, and a Pharisee as well! How completely he understood performance and self-righteousness. When he was persecuting the church, Paul believed he was doing a good work for God. He was sure that he was earning favor or merit with God by persecuting the Church! Yet in verse 8,

Paul expresses how the intimate knowledge he gained through his personal, intimate relationship with the Lord brought him out of righteousness by self-effort and, thus, to the Law of righteousness by faith—faith in the finished work of the Son.

In verses 9-11, Paul again emphasized that the only perfect righteousness was never attained by self-effort or works, but through faith in Jesus' perfect fulfillment of the Law for us at Calvary. We Believers also attain this resurrection of the dead (verse 11) by placing our faith in Romans 6:3-5.

In Philippians 3:12, Paul explicitly states that the righteousness provided for us through the sacrifice of God's Son is not sinless perfection, but a pursuing of all that Christ provided as we go forth (via the ministry of the Holy Spirit) to experience freedom from sinful domination.

GOD LOOKS AT THE HEART. HE IS NOT PUNITIVE. HE DOES NOT CONDEMN YOU.

Before this, like many Believers, Paul did not understand that God looks at the heart. You may be so bound up in a particular sin or bondage that you are committing that act day in and day out, sometimes for years on end, despising what you do, but feeling helpless, hopeless, or condemned. Remember, God looks at the heart. He is not punitive. He does not condemn you. You do that to yourself through ignorance of the liberty provided for you at the Cross (and Satan is very good at aiding you in such a belief or assessment) or through stubbornness, still trying to obtain the victory in your own strength and efforts—to no avail.

GOD GAVE HIS SON SO YOU COULD BE FREE. DON'T GIVE UP.

God looks at the heart—yours and mine—and He will never fail to answer the cry of a sincere heart. He loves you. God gave His Son so you could be free. Don't give up. If need be, confess your own inability to overcome that which is binding or harming you every day. Place your faith in Jesus and His finished work for you. Obey the following instructions:

Submit yourselves therefore to God. Resist the Devil, and he will flee from you.

—James 4:7

Acknowledge that your only hope (for the deliverance you need) is in Jesus Christ and His finished work. Then Satan will (if not immediately, then with your persistent faith and refusal to give up) flee from you. Why? Because you are essentially agreeing with God that all you will ever need, including this victory that seems impossible at the moment, was obtained for you at the Cross.

It was there that Satan and his kingdom were defeated and Believers were forever loosed from his power. Satan has no legal ownership of you any more. Remember, you now belong to another—the Lord Jesus. You are His bride.

This is how complete His work at Calvary is. When Jesus cried out, "It is finished," it truly was. It was ALL finished for you and me. God the Father acknowledged His Son's perfect substitutionary sacrifice for us in the resurrection.

Jesus rose from the dead. Death could no longer hold Him because the price had been paid for you and me. Had He not perfectly fulfilled the Law in His death, burial, and resurrection, we would still be bound by the chains of sin. But He rose victorious, and we rose with Him (positionally) to this new life where we now stand. It is God's will that each of His children experience this new life daily.

Again, it is the Holy Spirit's job to affect His will in us. Let Him. Rest in the Lord and trust in Him. It is okay to tell God you don't understand, but that you are placing yourself and all that concerns or burdens you in His loving hands, trusting that His Son's finished work is sufficient for you too. Ask God to lead you out of all that is hindering His Spirit's work, and He will do it.

ALL THE GRACE YOU WILL EVER NEED WILL BE GIVEN TO YOU.

Please realize that all the grace you will ever need will be given to you. It is a day-by-day dependence on Him, His Word, and His promises—all of which belong to Believers despite their experience. The following verses confirm this truth.

> *Do you think that the Scripture says in vain, The Spirit Who dwells in us lusts to envy? But He gives more Grace. Wherefore he said, God resists the proud, but gives Grace unto the humble.*
> —James 4:5-6

GOD GIVES GRACE THAT IS GREATER THAN OUR STRONGEST WEAKNESS.

We Are Weak but He Is Strong

Verse 5 tells Believers that the Holy Spirit wants control of all our thoughts, words, deeds, and actions. He truly wants to direct the course of our lives day by day and moment by moment; thus, He is envious of any control the sin nature exerts over Believers. You may be thinking, *How can this really be true for me? How can this be manifested in my life when I am so weak?*

It is true that we are weak in our own selves and always will be, but God gives grace that is greater than our strongest weakness.

It is when we realize our utter weakness and inability that we can truly be strong. Why? Only when we realize and acknowledge our inability to live the crucified life in our own efforts and strength (weakness) and yield to the Cross—where the power of our sin nature was forever broken as the reigning nature in us—is the Holy Spirit free to minister the grace and strength we need to daily live as those who were crucified with Him as brides of Christ.

Even Paul felt the futility of his own efforts and labor. In 2 Corinthians 12:9-10, Paul expounded on his most humbling experience that enabled him to see the weakness and corruptness of man's carnal nature and brought him to realize how much he needed God's strength. In verses 1 through 8, Paul shared his experience with the *thorn* that God allowed to buffet him in order to teach him about the corruptness of man's carnal nature. This process brought Paul to a place of humility that allowed him to experience freedom and victory through the grace provided by God in the finished work of His Son.

It is not expedient for me doubtless to glory. I will come to Visions and Revelations of the Lord. I knew a man in Christ above fourteen years ago, (whether in the body, I cannot tell; or whether out of the body, I cannot tell: God knows;) such an one caught up to the third Heaven. And I knew such a man, (whether in the body, or out of the body, I cannot tell: God knows;) How that he was caught up into Paradise, and heard unspeakable words, which it is not Lawful for a man to utter. Of such an one will I glory: yet of myself I will not glory, but in mine infirmities. For though I would desire to glory, I shall not be a fool; for I will say the truth: but now I forbear, lest any man should think of me above that which he sees me to be, or that he hears of me. And lest I should be exalted above measure through the abundance of the Revelations, there was given to me a thorn in the flesh, the messenger of Satan to buffet me, lest I should be exalted above measure. For this thing

I besought the Lord thrice, that it might depart from me. And he said unto me, My Grace is sufficient for you: for My strength is made perfect in weakness. Most gladly therefore will I rather glory in my infirmities, that the Power of Christ may rest upon me. Therefore I take pleasure in infirmities, in reproaches, in necessities, in persecutions, in distresses for Christ's sake: for when I am weak, then am I strong.

—2 Corinthians 12:1-10

In verse 8, we learn that Paul asked the Lord three times to remove the "thorn." Paul so wanted the "weakness" to be removed, but it did not happen. Have you cried out to God for such, yourself? I certainly have, and often more than three times! But the Lord's response was, "My grace is sufficient for you" (verse 9). The Lord is still saying that to you and me today.

In fact, as I progress in my walk with the Lord, I realize more and more how weak I am. Oh, how our flesh hates this revelation. Yet it is this very revelation and personal experience that the Lord uses to cause His children to depend more completely on Him, thereby infusing us with His strength—the very measure we need in every situation and circumstance we face.

Paul came to the place in his relationship with God that he could truly "glory in his infirmities or weaknesses" (verse 9b) so that Christ's power could be manifested in and through him. Paul realized that the humiliations suffered by his flesh were well worth the end result of God's gracious and merciful power resting in and upon him.

In fact, in verse 10 he explicitly says he took pleasure in these lessons and experiences because when he was weak, Paul was actually strong. It was when Paul acknowledged his weaknesses and inabilities that God's strength could rest upon him. This is God's desire for you and me too.

THE STRENGTH OF CHRIST IS MANIFESTED WHEN WE KNOW WE ARE WEAK.

He wants to be all we could ever need or desire but cannot be until we, like Paul, realize our utter inability to yield to His script, the way of the Cross. Remember,

God will not share His glory. The strength of Christ is manifested when we know we are weak. I pray this reality becomes more and more real to you and me as we go forth in greater revelation and understanding of God's grace and our human weakness.

God has not forgotten us. We are not the exception. In ourselves we Believers are forever weak and helpless, yet God has not abandoned us.

> *According as His Divine Power has given unto us all things that pertain unto life and Godliness, through the knowledge of Him Who has called us to Glory and Virtue.*
>
> —2 Peter 1:3

THERE IS NOTHING THAT THE ONE WHO KNOWS THE END FROM THE BEGINNING WILL NOT DO FOR HIS BELOVED BRIDES.

Everything we will ever need in our lifetime has been provided. God means what He says: EVERY-THING! This is the result of Christ's love, care, and protection of His brides. This is how much He loves us. There is nothing that the One Who knows the end from the beginning will not do for His beloved brides. The Lord already knows what lies ahead for each one of us and has made provision for us. He is there to shield and protect us and to command the angels on our behalf when He wills. Even though Jesus is not physically here with His brides (for the time being), He is still here in the hearts and lives of Believers through the Holy Spirit who indwells us. And, despite His absence *physically,* He is still able to keep His brides from stumbling or falling as they keep their faith in His finished work at Calvary.

> *Now unto Him Who is able to keep you from falling, and to present you faultless before the Presence of His Glory with exceeding joy—be Glory and Majesty, Dominion and power, both now and ever. Amen*
>
> —Jude 24-25

ASK GOD TO REVEAL MORE OF HIMSELF TO YOU, AND HE WILL.

What a promise!

To know more of Jesus' love for you, His bride, open your heart to Him more. Give Him time—or more time if you already spend time with Him—to fellowship with you. Let Him draw you closer to Him. Ask God to reveal more of Himself to you, and He will. Ask Him to remove all the obstacles—the hurts, wounds, lies, deceptions, and walls you may have erected—that prevent you from drawing closer to Him. Give up your erroneous belief that He wants to punish you, hurt you, or make you pay for your sins. Those are lies from the pit of hell.

If you are currently in a place of difficulty, please know that God is not condemning you, nor making you pay via whatever hurts or pains you. Remember, God allows the painful tests and trials to discipline us, to bring us to the very position Paul wrote about in 2 Corinthians 2:1-10. Jesus Christ cannot be more fully revealed in us until we reach the end of ourselves or hit the proverbial rock bottom. These hurtful, painful times (allowed by God) cause you and me to experience His overpowering strength, which can only be manifested as we experience and acknowledge our utter weakness.

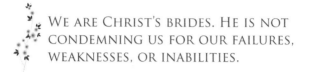

WE ARE CHRIST'S BRIDES. HE IS NOT CONDEMNING US FOR OUR FAILURES, WEAKNESSES, OR INABILITIES.

All chastening is for a season. It is not meant to hurt or punish you, as if God wants you knocked down before He will allow you to experience the blessings. No! No! No! Proverbs 3:12 says:

> *For whom the LORD loves He corrects; even as a father the son in whom he delights.*

He loves you. He loves me. We are the Father's children. We are Christ's brides. He is not condemning us for our failures, weaknesses, or inabilities. He knows we are but flesh, but we are slow in learning and accepting that.

Doesn't it help to know that Paul found himself in such a dilemma? This great man of faith had his faith struggles too. Life did not become easier for him after his conversion, but, oh, the victory he had. He found the answer to his struggle with sin and weakness, and he went on to live the victorious life God called him to as a bride of Christ.

GOD HAS ALWAYS USED *THORNS* TO TEST OR PROVE HIS PEOPLE.

God's Proving Process

In the first part of this chapter, I discussed Romans 7:1-6. Paul realized that as a Believer, he was no longer married to the Law but to Christ. In a later chapter of this book we will continue in Romans 7, learning that Paul's struggle with sin did not end with the realization of his marriage to Christ. He had much more to learn about his baptism into Christ, his marriage to Christ, and his carnal nature. And so do we! God has always used *thorns* to test or prove His people. We Believers and Paul are not unique. Look at the following example from the Old Testament.

Now these are the nations which the LORD left, to prove Israel by them, even as many of Israel as had not known all the wars of Canaan; only that the generations of the Children of Israel might know, to teach them war, at the least such as before knew nothing thereof; namely, five lords of the Philistines, and all the Canaanites, and the Sidonians, and the Hivites that dwelt in Mount Lebanon, from Mount Baal-hermon unto the entering in of Hamath. And they were to prove Israel by them, to know whether they would hearken unto the Commandments of the LORD, which He commanded their fathers by the hand of Moses.

—Judges 3:1-4

At this time, the Israelites were in Canaan, the Promised Land. God had rescued His people out of Egypt and commanded them to go in and possess the land of promise. Every provision was made for their victory, despite the *thorns* that remained in this land.

THIS PROVING IS ALWAYS FOR MAN'S BENEFIT SO HE MIGHT KNOW HIS TRUE CONDITION.

This younger generation of Israelites had not experienced the miracles their predecessors had, and now it was their turn to be proven. Would they serve the Lord or would they serve idols? Obviously, the Lord already knew their hearts (just as He knows ours). This proving is always for man's benefit so he might know his true condition.

In studying Judges 3:1-4, we see that God allowed five kings—five "thorns"—to remain in Canaan. Their purpose was to prove Israel and to teach the younger generation to depend on God's strength to obtain victory, as their forefathers had done. This younger generation had not yet learned the insufficiency of its own strength.

Remember, in accepting and acknowledging His weakness, Paul was made strong because he accepted God's way of strength and victory—the way of the Cross. Paul realized that his victory came in accepting the victory Christ won for us at the Cross, and he became separate unto God.

On the other hand, the Israelites had yet to be proven. They had to learn how to fight and win. Would they remain faithful to God during these difficult times? Judges 3:5-7 tells us what happened.

> *And the Children of Israel dwelt among the Canaanites, Hittites, and Amorites, and Perizzites, and Hivites, and Jebusites: and they took their daughters to be their wives, and gave their daughters to their sons, and served their gods. And the Children of Israel did evil in the sight of the LORD, and forgot the LORD their God, and served Baalim and the groves.*

The children of Israel did not remain separate unto God, but intermingled and intermarried with the occupants of these five nations, even serving their idol gods. In other words, they became assimilated into the lives and culture of these five heathen nations. Instead of honoring God as their source and strength, they sought to obtain their needs via their own efforts and methods.

What these Israelites did not realize was that God had allowed these five kings (and nations) to remain in their midst to prove and ultimately strengthen them. Technically, these five "thorns" were defeated foes. God wanted His people to seek Him in strategizing the necessary battles that really were victories as promised and given by Him. However, they went their own way, devising their own methods, and ultimately found themselves enslaved. Their idolatrous ways led to their slavery. Oh, how subtle the enemy is in attempting to divert the Believer's heart and focus from Christ and Him crucified to some other (idolatrous) focus.

Despite the Israelites' disobedience, God did not give up on them. And He does not give up on you or me! In verse 9 we learn that these children of Israel cried to the Lord, and He answered them with deliverance.

And when the Children of Israel cried unto the LORD, the LORD raised up a deliverer to the

Children of Israel, who delivered them, even Othniel the son of Kenaz, Caleb's younger brother.
—Judges 3:9

Any time Israel cried to the Lord, irrespective of their disobedience, God always heard their cry and delivered them. He is that same God today. If your heart is sincere as you cry out to Him, no matter what you may have done, He will hear and answer you.

You may have promised God a million times to stop committing a certain sin or to forsake an ungodly habit and failed miserably. You are not alone. That is why we are studying Romans 7, which explores the futility of man's efforts to overcome sin, even after becoming Believers. Paul, too, was confused regarding his seemingly endless struggle with sin until God gave him the revelation he sought.

So bear with me and do not be discouraged. You are reading this book because your heart cries out to the Lord to know more of Him, more of you, and more of your marriage as a Believer to Christ. Right now, He is wooing you back to Him. Run into His open arms. Let Him hold you, caress you, and wipe away your tears. Let Him show you how much He loves you right now.

He sees every heartbreak and every tear, and He feels your pain. He is there with you right now, even though you may not sense His Presence.

Tested and Tried—but Not Forsaken

This past year has been a year of deep waters and testing for us. Sometimes I felt as if I would be swallowed up, but as I looked to Him (and continue to look to Him) and confessed my own inability and helplessness, I learned more of trusting and resting in Him.

One year ago, my husband and I were on our way to Monaco, God's place of respite for us, enroute to my husband's conference in Cannes. We faced many difficulties shortly before our departure, and we were tempted to cancel our plans and forego God's script. Thank God, we chose to follow His plan. It was not easy, but in doing so, we received the needed rest and relaxation and, most of all, learned more about our loving, faithful God and ourselves.

As I reflect back on this year, I cannot believe how much our lives have changed. Not only with regard to the loss of Nathan and the addition of Nava to our lives, but also the seemingly endless times of testing and deep waters we and many of our close friends were called upon to endure.

How many times I have had to pick up my Bible or my first book and allow the Holy Spirit to direct me to the chapter, paragraph, verse, or sentence I needed right then! Truly God is answering my prayer, my cry, to know more of Him, more of me, more of the Cross, and more of being one of Christ's brides.

As I have said before, He never promised us a life without pain and sorrow, but He did promise to never leave nor forsake us and to be all we could ever need or want. All our answers are in Him.

This summer has been especially difficult while waiting for the serious injuries to my feet to heal and learning about fear and anxiety as I went through a time of testing, enriching, discipline, and correction—all while writing the first chapter of this book. I wondered at times if I would make it. Yes, some of it was due to the enemy's attacks or assaults, but not all of it. God is still in control, and Satan and his cohorts can do nothing (not a single thing) in my life (or yours) without God knowing it or allowing it.

Often, God allows these tests to show us the true condition of our hearts and the vileness and stubbornness of our flesh, which is in direct opposition to God.

Much of my wrestling has been my flesh warring against God, or wanting immediate resolutions to my many challenges. I wanted the tests to end right now. I was in rebellion against His prescribed course. Yet, in each situation, when I humbled myself before Him and yielded to His omniscience and sovereignty, I found the grace I needed to align myself with Him— the grace that allowed Him to bring my heart and will into one accord with Him.

How many times I have returned to the Cross—that empty Cross—and laid myself at His feet, realizing that all my cares, anxieties, fears, and worries had already been resolved by Him 2000 years ago.

I still return to "The Homestead" and the cross across the creek, where my first book was birthed. God still uses this visual aid setting to teach and correct me. He is ever-revealing more of Himself and more of my true self as I deny myself and take time to wait upon Him.

This past year, as many of my friends were also thrust into seemingly endless tests and deep waters, I wondered, *When will it all end. Will we make it? Will we come through victoriously?* I can tell you now that it ended, and we made it through victoriously! God did not forsake us.

I have learned more about the commitment of caring friends—friends who, like my husband and I, are "soldiers of the Cross." As these precious friends prayed and interceded for us while facing their own struggles and deep waters, God bound us all together in a very special way. Our friendships were strengthened, and our caring for each other deepened as we learned more about bearing one another's burdens.

> *Truly, the effectual fervent prayer of a Righteous man avails much.*
>
> —James 5:16b

We could not have survived this past year, and especially these past several months, without the love and care of such godly, righteous friends who prayed and interceded for us. God truly has increased this aspect of our lives and relationships. And He even restored relationships or friendships that seemed lost. How faithful He is in moving us back to Him. How amazingly He orchestrates the necessary conditions (our hearts and our wills, as well as timing) to bring forth His desired results. Often though, it is not our timetable but His that prevails. And how resistant or stubborn our flesh is—either demanding that He act more quickly or wait longer. And when we, like recalcitrant children, are not willing to submit to His script, we cry out, "No, Lord, You can't possibly mean that!"

As dear Mother Fludd says: "God doesn't work on our clock. He has His own. He has His own schedule, and none of us are going to change His mind." Furthermore, we will not receive all that His Son provided (no matter what our stage in this Christian walk) without obedience to His script.

If we refuse to lay down ourselves—our flesh, our "rights"—we will not experience the peace and freedom our souls need and desire. Stubbornness, refusal to forgive, refusal to reconcile, and self-righteousness impede God's work in our hearts and lives.

I learned so well during the past summer that this also includes fear, anxiety, and worry. I have come to realize that these three issues really express a lack of faith and trust in God and the power of His words and promises. But I have also learned that He is not punitive toward those who are caught up in these bondages. Often, we don't realize how deeply imbedded or ingrained such issues as fear, anxiety, and worry are in us until we cry out to Him for help, wait upon Him, and allow Him to reveal these deeply rooted spiritual issues.

Often we learned these responses simply because we grew up in homes or environments that taught and perpetrated them. Please note that this is not a license to blame parents. They were only living as they were taught and knew best. However, when we cry out to God with sincere hearts, He will lead us to the message of the Cross, where true freedom is found.

I wish it were as simple as instant revelation and instant resolution, but usually it is not so. But this is where faith and trust in a loving Abba Father—who knew us before we were born and only has our very best interests at heart—comes forth. It is a lifelong process of learning to trust Him, to rest in Him, and to rejoice in our salvation. And we do that one day at a time. Sometimes we need to just take time and deliberately re-focus our hearts and minds on the God Who so graciously and mercifully saved us and blessed us with His goodness. Sometimes intense or prolonged periods of testing can cause us to forget to thank God for those daily blessings that sustain us while we are in those deep waters.

Throughout these past months, as I allowed God to reveal my lack of trust in Him, I realized that part of His script for me is choosing to have a grateful heart. Yes, even as He unveiled the root of fear, with its horrible branches of anxiety, shame, worry, and depression, I learned that I can choose to be grateful.

I've learned to have a heart of gratitude for the things I had taken for granted. How many of us take time to thank God for our lives, our health, our jobs, our walks, our rides, and all His blessings? So often we take for granted such things as the sunshine, blue sky, fall colors, and freshly fallen snow. But we must never take for granted the salvation and deliverance that is ours because of Jesus, the Cross, and His shed Blood. When you're being tested, it is not easy to pull yourself up by the bootstraps and choose to be thankful and grateful to God, but you can do it. I know because I've done it.

While I was immersed in the tests and deep waters, I realized that my gratitude to God had slipped. And as I chose to be grateful, things started to change. That is why having my horse, Red, to carry me up those high hills at the barn and across the fields has been such a blessing these past several weeks. I am so grateful that God gave me such a trusty mount that seemed to sense my need, be it a cross-country trot or a relaxing walk. Those were special times that allowed me to pour out my fearful, anxious, worried heart to God, crying it out and then being still, allowing Him to comfort me, minister to me, teach me, and discipline me.

Despite the hell that seemed to be raging, I will never forget God's incredible Presence as I traversed the hills and fields of the classroom He uniquely fashioned just for me. And how grateful and thankful I am for Red, the mount God blessed me with twenty-one summers ago.

CHAPTER 3

THE ANCIENT LAND

TWO YEARS AGO WE WERE ENROUTE to Hong Kong on a sixteen-and-a-half-hour nonstop flight from New York's JFK airport. Sixteen-and-a-half hours! Yikes! How would I survive the flight? Eight years prior, we had made our first ministry jaunt to China, just three months after the British had returned Hong Kong to China. At that time, there were no nonstop flights from New York, so we flew to San Francisco and enjoyed a bit of R & R before flying on to Japan and China.

I was invited to minister in the New Territories, Sheung Shui, a university city, only two miles from the former Chinese border.

Hong Kong Island, Lantau Island, Kowloon, and the New Territories were returned to China in July 1997. Ministering there was such a wonderful experience for my husband and me. We stayed on Hong Kong Island, about midway up the incline to the renowned Victoria Peak. Our room, complete with a wall of windows, faced Victoria Harbour, and at times we felt as though we had been transported back to centuries ago. God truly fulfilled a dream of mine, and I could hardly believe I was trekking, walking, and hiking this beautiful and exciting country, let alone sailing across Victoria Harbour to Kowloon on the renowned Star Ferry.

During ministry days, the pastor's daughter met us at our hotel and took us to Sheung Shui via the Kowloon-Canton Railway. I never expected to see such beautiful scenery. The lush, green hills, with ancient villages scattered throughout, were so lovely. At times, I felt as if I were in the old Cary Grant movie that first introduced me to the beauty and wonders of that ancient land.

I was blessed with a wonderful and receptive congregation, and we witnessed the love and compassion of our loving God as He ministered to the people in body, soul, and spirit. Needless to say, we eagerly accepted the pastor's invitation to return and waited for God's timing.

That time came just two years ago—eight years after our first visit. While flying those sixteen-and-a-half hours, I eagerly awaited what God had planned for us on that trip. It was ministry, as well as a conference in Shanghai for my husband, and some R & R for us as well.

I managed to fall asleep for what I had hoped would be a long enough rest that only eight hours of the flight would remain when I awakened. But when I awoke, turned on my light, and looked at my watch, I realized that we had been airborne only four-and-a-half hours. That meant there were twelve more hours to go, instead of eight. A bored flight attendant noticed my light and came over to chat. One thing led to another, and before we knew it, we were back in the galley chatting about the Lord and praying. What an unexpected blessing that turned out to be. I shared my miracle testimony—telling about the God-orchestrated surgery that had cured me of a rare congenital heart defect—and talked about my ministry, especially since miracle. She talked about the couples' ministry she shared with her husband back in the Philippines. What a blessing for both of us.

A Room with a View

When we arrived on Kowloon, we stayed at the *grande dame* of hotels, where I had always wanted to stay. It truly reflects the old-world grandeur of bygone eras. And, again, God blessed us with a room with a view—almost an entire wall of glass facing Victoria Harbour. I must say, the formality of the hotel and staff was another treat for us. Despite its size, the hotel regularly hosts prominent world leaders, so security is very tight. We were known and addressed by name, and each floor had its own hotel staff to tend to any and all of the guest's needs. The staff introduced themselves to us, and inquired about how they could best serve us: which fruit we'd like in our fruit bowl every day, etc. And, to our amazement, if we left any clothing items out when we left our room, those items had been put away before we returned. I recall returning to our room one day to change shoes. I looked where I thought I had left them, but to no avail. I just knew I had not put them in the closet, but I opened the closet door and there they were, with all of our other shoes—arranged perfectly in a row.

I was amazed at how meticulously and joyfully the staff served the hotel guests. They truly wanted to please us. As I reflected on their servant spirit and my relationship with the Lord, I wondered, *How often do I really serve Him with joy, thanksgiving, and gratitude? Especially if things are not progressing as I think they should.* Hmmm.

 DEEP WATER TIMES ARE OPPORTUNITIES FOR GROWTH AS WE WAIT FOR HIM TO FULFILL HIS PROMISES TO MEET OUR EVERY NEED.

We rekindled our relationship with the pastor and his family, and I gave my miracle testimony at his church, which was still in Sheung Shui but in a new and lovely facility. I also saw a friend I had met on our first trip, and it was really nice to see her and her family again.

Those sixteen-and-a-half hours of patiently waiting to arrive were well worth it—though I often wondered if we would ever get to Chek Lap Kok, Hong Kong's new airport on Lantau Island. Isn't our walk with God sometimes like that? Patiently waiting and waiting; then wondering. It is hard to sit still and enjoy God's *flight plan*, especially if the ride or flight is not what we anticipated or hoped for. Oh, these times of testing and growing can be arduous. These are the *deep water* times when we are given opportunities for growth as we wait for Him to fulfill His promises to meet our every need and to never fail or forsake us. He will go with us and, essentially, be our rest and Peace, if we will just trust in Him and believe Him, especially during the turbulence.

Why do we become fearful and anxious when we know that God already has the circumstances of our lives worked out? He certainly has not changed His mind about us—or about what He has already given or willed to us. But, often, like the Israelites, we are not satisfied with the day's manna He provides. We want all the manna now so we won't have to continue to wait upon Him, trust in Him, and rest in Him.

Why are we still fighting battles that He has already won for us? Remember, Jesus paid the price for our salvation and freedom 2000 years ago at the Cross. Our loving Lord, our Husband, has already provided for our every need. So what keeps us from knowing and experiencing the reality of it? It is a matter that must be addressed in prayer:

> *Lord, open the eyes of our hearts—open the eyes of our understanding too. Unveil any lies, deceptions, or bondages that we are still serving regarding us and You. Show us any hindrances that are preventing us from receiving what You have for us and remove them.*
>
> *Show us, too, that what You have allowed, You can work out for us. Knowing what You knew about us then and what You know about us now, You still sent your Son to die for us. Wow! Thank You, Lord.*

 THE BOOK IS CLOSED. NO LONGER DOES GOD COUNT OUR SINS AGAINST US.

No Longer in Bondage

The past is truly past. We are really free. We are no longer in bondage—no longer who or what we used to be. The book is closed. No longer does God count our sins against us. There is nothing more to remember—nothing left to pay for. So why do we succumb to the enemy's bait? Why do we replay over and over again a sin or sins that cause us so much pain? If God declares them perfectly atoned for and doesn't remember them, why do we? This only keeps us in a prison, unable to be free. Unable to receive His compassion that says, "I won't fail or forsake you, despite what you have done."

It is in knowing God's love for us that the strongholds of the enemy are broken and no longer have the power to bind or rule us. We must learn to accept the truth that we are accepted by the Father just as we are. All of those old roots of perfectionism—being better, trying harder—will no longer stand. It is in knowing and accepting that we are loved and accepted by God that we are free to love, accept, and forgive ourselves, as well as others, without demanding payment from us or them.

 GOD'S COMPASSION HEALS AND RESTORES US, EVEN AFTER WE HAVE IGNORED HIS WARNING: "DON'T DO THAT."

Remember, as Believers, we belong to Him, and so do our problems. He is our Answer. He is the Master Physician, Surgeon, Miracle-worker, Problem-solver, and HEALER.

God disciplines and corrects us out of love. God's compassion heals and restores us, even after we have ignored His warning: "Don't do that." God is not out to get you or me for our failure to listen and obey. Yes, there can be consequences, but in His mercy, He not only forgives us, but heals us as well. He does not plan heartbreak and defeat in order to punish us. Yet how many of us have found ourselves serving this lie at one time or another? The enemy delights in taunting us with his "It's too late—you've been disobedient and gone too far" lies. Remember, God did not require us to change before He forgave us! We could never earn or merit what He has already ordained for us. All has been freely given to us because of the finished work of His Son at the Cross.

Remember, God has already forgiven you for the sins that you re-live over and over again. So why do you cause yourself so much pain? Forgive yourself. Ask God to help you so your healing and restoration can begin. It isn't easy when you have taken a hard fall, but He is not the one reminding you of it over and over, forcing you to review the evidence. All has been forgiven, atoned for, and washed in the precious BLOOD of Jesus. By refusing to accept this, we act as gods, declaring that we know better than the one true God. The freedom that is ours in the Son cannot come unless we are in accord with the Master Who said:

> *Neither do I condemn you, go, and sin no more.*
>
> —John 8:11

And, which is easier to say?

> *Your sins be forgiven you*

or...

> *Arise, and walk.*
>
> —Matthew 9:5

Do you realize that Jesus essentially took our personal history (yours and mine) and made it His? Obviously, He did not live our lives, but in becoming our perfect Substitute, the iniquity of us all was laid on Him. All of our sins were lifted out of us and carried away by Jesus who became that perfect sin-offering for you and me. And that perfect work of Jesus provided for our mental and emotional healing too. We now have freedom from mental anguish, despair, disappointments, and hopelessness. All of this He did for His brides.

His Word tells us:

> *Therefore if any man be in Christ, he is a new creature: old things are passed away; behold, all things are become new.*
>
> —2 Corinthians 5:17

Becoming New Creatures

The literal Greek says "all things are becoming new." Doesn't that make you feel better? If we examine our daily lives, they hardly reflect the "are become new" part of that powerful verse. The English language often does not adequately or correctly express the Hebrew or Greek texts. So if we Believers are in the process of becoming new, then we must recognize that "being in Christ," as one of His brides, is a process. Too often we expect instantaneous progression and growth; then we fall into condemnation, guilt, or shame when our lives exhibit otherwise.

GOD WILL DELIVER US IN THE TEST OR TRIAL OR OUT OF IT.

If you feel like you are on a sixteen-and-a-half-hour flight with more turbulence than you ever expected or imagined, don't despair. God is still in control, and He does not allow anything in your life or mine without His knowledge and consent. God will deliver us in the test or trial or out of it. It is His call, not ours, and He truly has our best interests at heart. All He does and all He allows in our lives are out of His love for you and me.

Yes, that can be difficult to acknowledge when you seem to be hopelessly bound and unable to get out of the fire. But that is when faith and patience enter in. It is difficult to stand your ground and wait when you seem to go two steps forward then three or four backward. And it is difficult to pray for someone to be healed and rejoice when they are healed (sometimes instantaneously), while you wait and wait and wait for your own healing. But God does not love us any less, and He doesn't withhold His answers, thinking we need to experience more failure or heartbreak before He grants our prayers. No. That kind of thinking is a lie from the pit of hell. Yet how many of us, when we are weary, tired, and disappointed, succumb to the enemy's taunts? Our flesh wants the answer now, and we often divert our focus from the Lord and His promises when the answer does not come when we think it should. Has He not promised? Then it is so. Why? Because we see and experience it now? NO! Because He, God, said so, and He cannot lie.

As I write this chapter, I am still waiting for the healing of my injury, the healing of my feet. It has been difficult, especially after appearing to be "home free" only to suffer setbacks. When I recall the healing miracles God has allowed me to witness under the ministry He gave me, as well as personal healings in my own body, my human nature so wants my feet to be healed and restored right now. My flesh hates to wait. But I also think of what a witness my healing would be to my care providers and others I know. What an opportunity it would be for them to witness God's wisdom and power that supersedes man's skills and abilities. But despite the waiting, and the pain and anguish, I know that God has never failed me yet.

> HIS LOVE, MERCY, AND FAITHFULNESS REMINDS ME THAT IT IS ALL BECAUSE OF WHO HE IS AND BECAUSE OF HIS GREAT LOVE FOR ME.

I know that He will provide for all my daily needs, and that I'll be fine as we travel. It isn't easy, but I still heed His call and do my best to fulfill His will, as I lean on Him and step out in faith (sometimes with extreme pain). Sometimes I feel completely devoid of faith, and yet I witness His love, mercy, and faithfulness—and He reminds me that it is all because of who He is and because of His great love for me.

Do I still get fearful at times? Do I worry at times? YES—and then I go back to the One I left and surrender my anguished heart to Him once again. I ask Him to expose any fear, worry, doubt, unbelief, and anxiety that may be hindering His plan for my life. Now, all of these harmful emotions were defeated at the Cross, so why do we worry, fret, and fear? It is because we don't really trust Him, His Word, and His promises. We often think we know a better way, and we want to "help" Him direct our course. Instead of learning to trust God and rest in Him, we wrestle with Him!

If you are facing such struggles, don't despair. Neither you nor I were the first or last to wrestle with God. When our routines are altered, even temporarily, we want to know God's script for the whole process right now. We do not want to wait on the One Who alone knows the script and reveals what He chooses when He is ready. But God knows best, and it benefits us to rest in, trust, and wait upon Him one day at a time.

Remembering Words of Wisdom

I think of Sister Fludd, who said, "God doesn't work on our time." And my friend Lorraine S., who said, "It is not a Burger King mentality of 'having it your way.'" Yes, it must be God's way, and this is only achieved when we cease our struggling and wrestling and let Him be God.

How humbling. Years ago as a newlywed student, I had no thoughts of foot injuries or problems, let alone having a fifth chamber in my heart. I was a new bride involved with my studies and university Christian groups, and I was full of joy and excitement. Oh, how little we know as young brides, both in the natural as well as brides of Christ. But as we grow in the Lord, life gets tougher.

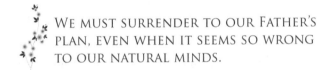

WE MUST SURRENDER TO OUR FATHER'S PLAN, EVEN WHEN IT SEEMS SO WRONG TO OUR NATURAL MINDS.

Our loving Father permits tests, uniquely fashioned for each of us, that sometimes shake us as we enter our world. Even though we may not understand it, this is love Himself providing just what we need to strengthen our faith. The proper response is to obediently accept that which hurts and exposes our true hearts and flesh—and to run to our Husband and cleave unto Him for new strength. Once again, the words, "When I am weak, then am I strong" take on new meaning.

I think of my friend Elloree, who said, "All we have to do is walk it out." We must surrender, submitting to our Father's plan, even when it seems so wrong to our natural minds. We must wait for Him to give the day's marching orders—not moving until we have His script or plan.

During my time of testing, my friend Shirley faithfully reminded me to look at the higher facts and promises of God's Word, which supersede natural wisdom or facts. Another friend, Lorraine L., reminded me that the enemy is just doing his job, but he cannot and will not succeed if we cleave to the promises of God. I realized that I cleave to those promises because I cleave to the One Who is behind those promises—the One Who breathed life into His very words and stands behind them. The One Who is wooing His children and His Son's brides to stand fast and not lean on their own understanding—acknowledging Him in all their ways, and ignoring the natural facts or circumstances—will direct their cause.

IF HE SAID IT, IT IS SO, AND HE WILL DO WHAT HE SAID. IN HIS MIND IT IS ALREADY DONE.

Wait—wait—trust. It is really difficult to do that at times, isn't it? These times reveal the impatience of our flesh. How conniving we can be, trying to manipulate God. Or if that doesn't work (and, of course, it NEVER does), then trying to manipulate others in attempts to obtain the results or answers we desire or believe God promised us. If He promised it, then hold on and don't let go. If He said it, it is so, and He will do what He said. In His mind it is already done. Again, all that we will ever need was provided 2000 years ago through the sacrifice of God's Son.

But we want it now, huh?

My friend Martha reminded me of the many miracles surrounding the healing of my heart problem and encouraged me to believe for another miracle for my current situation. She also echoed Teresa and Deb, who assured me that God doesn't allow or give us more than we can bear. Hmmm. How easily our flesh can forget this when things don't progress as we planned! I remind myself that my loving God is with me here, right now, in the midst of this seemingly endless storm. He knows my pains, hurts, and tears—and He knows yours too.

I think of Alleyne, my best friend and "sister," with whom I have shared almost all of my adult life. We just marvel at what God has done—and continues to do—in our lives. Our relationship with each other has been strengthened, and our fellowship with God has deepened, especially as we have weathered the storms and cruel blows of life.

Kathy reminds me to be bold and strong in God—to push forward, knowing that the Lord my God is with me. And, my loving husband, Dan, ever-reminds me of the love, compassion, and faithfulness of our God. He truly exemplifies, in the natural, the husband who tends to, cares for, and protects his bride. He is ever-encouraging me, especially when progress slows and seems to reverse. During my times of wavering, he reminds me to return to the Cross and see my situation in light of the finished work of Jesus at the Cross. I have learned that when I do that, then there is nothing—nothing—to fear. How He tends to His wounded ones, inviting us back into His arms and encouraging us to sit at the place of victory—the Cross.

God placed so many other loving friends and prayer partners in our lives for this time of struggle.

We have experienced such love, as never before, as these wonderful friends and prayer partners continue to pray, encourage, lift us up, and refuse to let go—all declaring that it is their time to do for Dan and me as we, in times past, have done for them. After all, this is what genuine relationships of love are all about. Love compels us to pray for one another, care for one another, share with one another, and to go through life upholding one another as our various times of trial by fire emerge.

In chapter 2 I spoke of the need for a grateful and thankful heart, and, especially for the daily blessings we often take for granted. I encourage you to look beyond your current natural circumstances and recall what God has done for you in the past. Being thankful and grateful really does bring forth joy, hope, and a change of attitude.

 OUR LOVING LORD DESIRES THAT HIS BRIDES BE ALIGNED, IN ONE ACCORD WITH HIM.

Aligning the Natural with the Supernatural

As we continue to yield our hearts, minds, and wills to God—especially during the tough and enigmatic (to us humans) times—He will reposition us and allow our uncomfortable situations to draw us closer to Him. We become more closely aligned with Him when we desire to have that which is hindering His will in our lives removed. A chiropractor seeks to align one's spine in order to bring the body back to its normal position. In this way, the various parts of one's body will perform optimally. Any of you who use the services of a chiropractor know that this process, most often, is not instantaneous. The body wants—and often screams for—the old and familiar as it learns to accept a new alignment that allows healing and helps prevent further injury or problems. How much more our loving Lord desires that His brides be aligned, in one accord with Him, so that which has been hindering His perfect will for us can be removed. When we see Him in light of His finished work at the Cross, it becomes easier to rest in Him and His love and to accept the victory He has already won for us.

You may be thinking, *Is there really hope for me? Have I gone so far that His grace and mercy will now be withheld from me?* Again, the enemy whispers (or sometimes screams): "It is too late. You didn't obey and learn your lesson(s), so God is now withholding that which He willed for your situation." No! No! No! Not only is God the God of second chances, but He is the God of many, many chances. He knows the anguish of your heart, and He knows that you sincerely long for His will.

God really knows our hearts. Unlike humans who judge others by their outward actions or circumstances, our Father judges us by the condition of our hearts. He knows the one who is still bound and, for whatever reason(s), is unable to find the promised deliverance, victory, or healing. If God cares about a fallen sparrow (Matthew 10:29), how much more does He care about you and me? So often man is confused or ignorant about God and the Cross, so he attempts to earn or merit God's favor and blessing(s), which is an effort in futility because Jesus obtained healing, deliverance, and victory for each of His brides at the Cross. Yes, many of us have sat under doctrine that is in direct opposition to the message of the Cross, but because our hearts are sincere—though sincerely wrong at times—God hears the cries of our hearts and directs us to the true message of the Cross, where our answers are found. Remember, the Lord Himself is our answer. He is all we could ever want or need, and all we will ever need is found in Him. Wow!

When we come to know Him as He really is, fear drops away. It is in knowing Him and His character that we can trust Him and not be afraid when He says, "Fear not." He sometimes allows times so dark and bleak that we cannot sense His Presence so our faith can be strengthened in the One Who said:

> *For I the LORD thy God will hold thy right hand, saying unto thee, Fear not; I will help thee.*
> —Isaiah 41:13

The following scriptures give us insight about the importance of God's Presence and grace:

> *And he [Esau] said unto him [Jacob], My lord knows that the children are tender, and the flocks and herds with young are with me: and if men*

should overdrive them one day, all the flock will die. Let my lord, I pray you, pass over before his servant: and I will lead on softly, according as the cattle that goes before me and the children be able to endure, until I come unto my lord unto Seir. And Esau said, Let me now leave with you some of the folk who are with me. And he [Jacob] said, There is no need! let me find grace in the sight of my lord.

—Genesis 33:12-15

Seek God's Presence

Jacob approached God for his petition on the basis of God's grace, not his own merit. As I said before, this is our only way of receiving and experiencing His grace in our own lives. God's grace comes only through the finished work of the Son. Note that in verse 15, Jacob was reluctant to go forward. He was displaying the traits of Moses, who said, "If Your Presence go not with me, carry us not up hence" (Exodus 33:15). After all that the Israelite nation had been through, Moses was unwilling to continue in his quest for the Promised Land unless God's Presence accompanied him. That should be our desire and prayer too.

The apostle Paul gives us this instruction:

Let your conversation be without covetousness; and be content with such things as you have: for He has said, I will never leave you, nor forsake you.

—Hebrews 13:5

I remind you, again, the literal Greek says, "He Himself has said…" The Lord, your Husband, personally promised this to His brides.

And what about Psalm 121? Oh, I have meditated and prayed this so often.

I will lift up my eyes unto the hills, from whence comes my help. My help comes from the LORD, which made Heaven and Earth. He will not suffer your foot to be moved: He Who keeps you will not slumber. Behold, he Who keeps Israel shall neither slumber nor sleep. The LORD is your keeper: the LORD is your shade upon your right hand. The sun shall not smite you by day, nor the moon by night. The LORD shall preserve you from all evil: he shall preserve your soul. The LORD shall preserve your going out and your coming in from this time forth, and even for evermore.

—Psalm 121

AS WE ABIDE IN HIM, HE WILL KEEP US FROM EVIL AND PRESERVE OUR SOUL.

Our help comes from the One Who made all of heaven and earth. Verses 3 and 4 promise His constant care and protection as we anchor ourselves to Him and His Word. If the Lord does not slumber or sleep, then His loving care and watchful eye are continuous, unceasing! In verse 5 we are told that God Himself will protect our strength. The "right hand of God" refers to the strength of God. In verse 6 the Lord tells us He will not allow His Creation to work against us, but for us. Verse 7 tells us that as we abide in Him and anchor ourselves in the finished work of the Son, He will fulfill His promise to keep us from evil and preserve our soul. And, in verse 8, we see that God means all of this to be for us at all times. Our Lord, our Husband, is a "covering" for His brides.

You may be filled with joy and hope right now, while others are still believing a lie—"But I can't believe or hope anymore because I've failed Him so many times." We will always fail if our faith is in anyone or anything other than Jesus Christ and Him crucified. But God is not the author of your condemnation, guilt, or shame. The Holy Spirit convicts, but He does not condemn. Satan is the one who condemns, orchestrating scripts that lure defeated Believers to condemnation, guilt, and shame. How easily we can forget one of my favorite scriptures:

> *There is therefore now no condemnation to them which are in Christ Jesus, who walk not after the flesh, but after the Spirit.*
>
> —Romans 8:1

 GOD, WHO KNOWS THE END FROM THE BEGINNING, (ISAIAH 46:10) ALREADY KNOWS WHAT WE HAVE DONE (OR WILL DO) FOR OUR ENTIRE LIVES!

Satan wants to see Believers entrapped in hopelessness and despair. He wants you to believe that God is so disgusted with you or disappointed in you that He has forsaken you or given up on you. But, remember God, who knows the end from the beginning, (Isaiah 46:10) already knows what we have done (or will do) for our entire lives! And despite that, He still loved us enough to send His Son to die for us. He loves us so much that He wants us to receive all that He has ordained for us. Yes, He loves us that much.

Remember, Satan accuses and condemns with the intent of bringing Believers to a state of hopelessness, whereas the Holy Spirit convicts with the intent of bringing Believers to repentance and hope. Our Father and Lord wants to have fellowship with us. That is why part of the Holy Spirit's ministry is to connect and lead repentant Believers back into fellowship with God. God created each one of us for fellowship and relationship with Him, and He continues to love us even as we resist Him (and His script) or wrestle with Him.

In the next chapter we will discuss Job. Despite Job's assessment of his situation and his very human responses, God never failed, forsook, or abandoned him, even when he questioned God and complained against Him. Through all the hellish experiences, God was there with Job every step of the way, and Job experienced a victory and triumph that he never could have imagined.

As my husband and I wait upon God during our test and "trial by fire," I, too, am reminded of the victory and triumph that Job experienced. Is it easy? No! In fact, it is more difficult now than it was many months ago. We would not have made it this far had it not been for the faithfulness, mercy, and grace of God—and the love and faithfulness of so many wonderful friends with whom we are knitted or fashioned together as a "many-braided" cord.

I am so glad we booked that sixteen-and-a-half-hour nonstop flight to Hong Kong two years ago. Blessings that I had not expected or anticipated made that trip "a la" (likened to) another of my favorite verses from Ephesians:

> *Now unto Him who is able to do exceeding abundantly above all that we ask or think, according to the power that works in us—Unto Him be Glory.*
>
> —Ephesians 3:20-21

One of the neatest blessings was rendezvousing with Yukiko, my good Christian friend who I had not seen in almost seven years. She flew into Hong Kong from Japan and spent a day and night with me while my husband was at a conference in Shanghai.

From the moment we embraced in the hotel lobby until "lights out" that night, it was nonstop talking and laughing, with a lot of walking. It was as if all those years had never separated us. Each of us confessed that we had wondered what it would be like to be together again after all these years. Of course, God knew it would be a wonderful time that we would never forget.

At night, back in our hotel room, Yukiko and I were like coeds in a luxurious dorm room. Sharing, laughing, and seemingly nonstop conversation—much of it about the Lord, the focus in both our hearts and lives.

Even as we traversed the streets of Kowloon, the "hagglers" could not interrupt our conversation. When we finally decided it was time to sleep, we left the wall of glass uncovered so we could experience the breathtaking beauty of Victoria Harbour and Hong Kong Island at night. God truly did more for us than we could have asked or imagined. And He still does, today, no matter what our present situation or circumstance may be.

I am so grateful Dan and I took that sixteen-and-a-half-hour flight!

CHAPTER 4

THE REFLECTING LAKE

As I ENTERED OUR FAMILIAR SUITE ON the waterfront of this peaceful, placid lake, I felt God's Peace and Presence welcome and envelope me. It had been one year since we were last here, and, oh, how things have changed.

One year ago, I was writing chapter four of my first book in this very suite. Nathan, our beloved English Setter was with us, and my husband and I so looked forward to the respite we so desperately needed after an especially intense several months.

I longed for more time alone with God, away from life's intense and hectic pace. And, as usual, He did not disappoint me. I left this Olympic village after Christmas last year with a greater love and understanding of God, my Father, and of Jesus and what His finished work of the Cross means.

Little did we know what 2007 held for us. But God did, and He has been here with us every step of the way.

I walked into our suite—and into God's arms. Yes, the lake and surrounding mountains are so peaceful. I feel a world away from life back home. I feel protected from that which would attempt to disturb or steal the inner peace that has been increasing since we left home.

Mirror Lake—a time for reflecting—a time for further growth and advancement in my walk with Him. A time for resting, instruction, and going further in my walk and relationship with God than I had ever dared before.

I expected to return, as in the years before, needing time away from my hectic pace, wanting and desiring more quality time with the Lord and with my husband.

And taking advantage of God's created beauty—the crisp, cold, pristine air and beautiful mountains—and enjoying time together—Pat, Dan, and Nathan.

This time, it is just Pat and Dan. We almost brought Nava with us, but she is a young and very rambunctious puppy. Due to my injury and all that has evolved, Dan felt we needed to be alone so more healing could take place. Deep down, I knew it, too, although I had made reservations at a local kennel so Nava could spend some time there and some time here with us. But in the two or three days preceding our departure, God made it clear that He needed our undivided attention back here.

As I write this chapter, I am ensconced in His Peace and His Presence. It is almost as if I can forget about my injury—all the hurt, heartbreak, uncertainly, and stress. I have had to endure burning pain that I never knew existed and a myriad of tests—all with normal results. There are no explanations for the months of severe physical discomfort, but I am learning some intense lessons about God's compassion and mercy. I'm also enjoying the support of a many-braided cord of wonderful friends who won't let me give up.

Unfortunately, there have also been some lessons in human nature's self-righteous side—well-meaning friends who behaved like Job's friends. I truly understand how Job must have felt as his friends pierced him to the core.

These past months have been so long. I thought I would be totally healed in two months. Yes, the doctors said foot injuries take a long time to heal. I was told to expect six to nine months for healing due to the severity of the injury. But I seemed to progress so quickly those first few weeks. Only God knows what happened, and only He knows what is taking place now in the spiritual realm. Believe me, I am well aware that this battle or test is spiritual, despite the physical manifestations. I have never been so aware of Satan's desire to destroy me spiritually, mentally, emotionally, and physically. The attacks were so strong at times that I wanted to give up.

I wondered if God heard my cries, and yes, I have wondered why. Lack of sleep due to pain and stress still wears me out sometimes. I find myself just fighting to survive. And to further complicate matters, my inability to tolerate most medicines seriously limits my options. Truly, this has been a test of faith such as I have never experienced.

WE MUST TRUST HIM AND WALK THROUGH THE FIRE WITH HIM IF WE ARE TO EXPERIENCE HIS ESCAPE PLAN.

Having my life so suddenly and unexpectedly altered seriously challenges my faith. But I have spent a lot of time studying and meditating on God's Word. The Holy Spirit led me to study two Old Testament books, Joshua and Job, both of which have greatly ministered to me during this difficult time. He also led me to a study of the New Testament book of Revelation to remind me of how fleeting human life is here on earth, and how limitless eternity with our Lord will be for Believers who are Christ's brides.

Although I believe that God does not allow us to experience more than we can bear—and that He always provide His way of escape—I have learned that we must trust Him and walk through the fire with Him if we are to experience His escape plan—His victory for us.

> *There has no temptation taken you but such as is common to man: but God is faithful, who will not suffer you to be tempted above that ye are able; but will with the temptation also make a way to escape, that you may be able to bear it.*
>
> —1 Corinthians 10:13

 I WONDERED WHERE GOD WAS AND IF HE WAS SO DISGUSTED WITH ME THAT HE HAD WITHDRAWN HIS HAND FROM ME.

It wasn't so hard to trust and believe Him those first couple of months, but the unceasing pain and lack of sleep took its toll, and the enemy temporarily had me in a vice grip. I wondered where God was and if He was so disgusted with me that He had withdrawn His hand from me. Yes, this from the woman who wrote *The Cross of Christ: One Woman's Perspective*—the very woman who teaches from the book of Hebrews:

> *Let your conversation be without covetousness; and be content with such things as ye have: for he hath said, I will never leave thee, nor forsake thee.*
>
> —Hebrews 13:5

This woman—who ministered Hebrews 13:5, along with the love, compassion, and mercy of God to others—felt abandoned or rejected by God.

In partial (not total) defense of myself, I should mention that I finally (after four months of horrible burning pain) agreed to try what my doctor called a "granny dose" of medicine. Even one-half of this "granny dose" altered my mind and impaired my ability to think clearly or function as I attempted to go through my days, with limited mobility. And, should you be wondering—this medication is the mildest in its class.

My whole being was consumed with feelings—physical, emotional, and mental—like I had never experienced, and I realized that my ability to pray was hampered. This was when I realized that I had to be more dependent on God—in ways I'd never had to before—if I wanted to survive. Yes, my husband, our friends, and I prayed about the physicians' prognosis and advice, crying out to God that we would not miss His script.

GOD HAS BEEN USING WHAT SATAN MEANT FOR MY DESTRUCTION TO WORK FOR MY GOOD.

Surviving the trauma of my near-death experience caused from my heart problem was very difficult, but this experience has been worse. The spiritual warfare is much more intense, and so is the resistance of my flesh to God's ultimate purpose in allowing this fiery trial. Oh, I have learned a lot about God, the enemy, and human nature (the flesh)—and not just the human nature or flesh of my "Job friends" but my own flesh as well. Yes, my own flesh wrestles with God because of the length and intensity of this test, but my flesh must be surrendered to the Cross if I am to progress to His very best for me.

All along, God has been using what Satan meant for my destruction to work for my good—but, oh, the resistance of the flesh. I finally realize that God knows my heart. He knows there is substance within me (that I don't even recognize) that He can and will use if I will walk through this fire with Him. I am. I have made a quality decision to walk this walk as long as He is at my side.

If our faith is to grow, the Lord must allow situations or circumstances that will challenge our current level of faith. Satan may have marked me for destruction, but God has marked me for victory. My job is to believe God and turn a deaf ear to Satan, my "Job friends," and man's wisdom that contradicts God's Word or doctrines of demons. And this is also your job when you are presented with such a fiery challenge or test.

Praise God for our many friends who heeded God's call to intercede for me, especially when I was so broken, both physically and emotionally. Their love and care for Dan and me is beyond words. It is the love of God expressed through surrendered vessels extended to one of His wounded, hurting children. They truly are walking through this with me, even though I am the only one physically experiencing all of it. This is a love we've never experienced. We truly thank and praise God for our friends' faithfulness to Him. If they refuse to give up, how much more determined is our loving Lord!

Forgiving Myself

I am learning more about forgiveness too—God's forgiveness toward me, even when I ignore His voice, and the need to forgive myself for ignoring His voice. Until recently I really had not forgiven myself for resisting God's script for this time in my life.

IF GOD FORGAVE ME, HOW CAN I DO LESS?

I realized that in refusing to forgive myself, I was, essentially, saying that Jesus' finished work at the Cross was not sufficient for me in this case, thus cutting myself off from the benefits of the Cross. I was tying God's hands, and Satan loves that. Well, *no more*. If God forgave me, how can I do less? Did this reality come easily? No. The enemy had a stronghold on me in this area, but as I cried out to God, He answered me. He cut through some strong cords of wrong beliefs that were deeply imbedded in me from previous erroneous teaching and experiences that were a part of my upbringing.

Some of these roots can be very thick and deep! I did not realize, despite my teaching, that God is not punitive, deep down. There were still some roots in me that caused me to think otherwise. I still felt that I needed to pay for that which Jesus had already paid. I had, unknowingly, in my personal salvation, confused accepting responsibility with "payment required."

JESUS PAID THE PRICE—THE PENALTY—
SO WE CAN FREELY MOVE BEYOND SIN.

Jesus paid the price—the penalty—so we can freely move beyond sin to the love, mercy, and grace of God that allows Him to work what Satan meant for evil into something good and precious to God. Now I finally understand what author and teacher Malcolm Smith meant when he said God will take the "manure" of a situation and turn it into "fertilizer." I discovered that my sin had to be pardoned, wiped out, and forgotten forever so God could use the situation for His glory and my good.

Remember, the Bible refers to Satan as the accuser of the brethren, and, thus, the accuser of the brides of Christ. His job is to accuse us before God's throne day and night.

> *And I heard a loud voice saying in Heaven, Now is come Salvation, and Strength, and the Kingdom of our God, and the power of His Christ: for the accuser of our Brethren is cast down, which accused them before our God day and night.*
> —Revelation 12:10

ONE DOCTOR ACTUALLY TOLD ME THAT I NEEDED TO DO EXACTLY WHAT I TEACH!

God's Guiding Presence

As I struggled with my trauma, I allowed myself to succumb to Satan's torments. Yet God was—and is—always in control, never allowing him to do more than He ordains.

I repeatedly relived the accident, especially when I was at my weakest point, but this was not God's will—it was Satan's. One doctor actually told me that I needed to do exactly what I teach! He told me that I needed to do what I wrote in my first book! He was essentially telling me that I was the woman of faith who wrote that book, not the one who presented before him that day!

Not surprisingly, my husband and I had prayed that this doctor would only say and do what God directed. Well, he sure did. When he entered the examination room, he told me that life is a series of tests and that our faith cannot grow without tests (tests are designed to increase our faith and strengthen us). He told me that my current test involved surrendering fear, doubt, anxiety, and stress to God. I had to believe that I would heal and get better. And he was so right. Fear, doubt, anxiety, and stress had definitely invaded my life and held court as the months progressed.

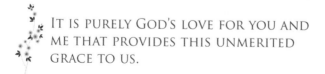

IT IS PURELY GOD'S LOVE FOR YOU AND ME THAT PROVIDES THIS UNMERITED GRACE TO US.

Granted, none of us deserve to be forgiven. It is purely God's love for you and me that provides this unmerited grace to us—this forgiveness for all of our sins for all time—past, present, and future.

How many have fallen into a trap similar to mine, with this god-like arrogance that says, "But I knew better. I don't deserve to be forgiven, so I will have to pay for all of the ungodly things I've done." Why do we do this when we know that Jesus paid for all that 2000 years ago? Yet if we refuse His shed Blood, as well as the stripes on His back (see Isaiah 53:4-5 with commentary), we will remain in self-imposed bondage.

Don't you think He knew I would have the accident? And, don't you think He knew He could bring me through? He knows each of our hearts and will use these situations in our lives to move us beyond what we can imagine, if we will walk through this fire with Him.

GOD WANTS ALL OF YOU AND HE WANTS ALL OF ME.

So don't give up on yourself. To do so is to disavow the finished work of the Son. Is this easy to do when you are in the middle of such a test or challenge? No.

Especially when you seem to take two steps forward and one, two, or three back. Okay, you can remain stagnant, with seemingly no progress at all. But if you cry out to God, and keep crying out to Him—even when your cries seem to fall upon deaf ears—He will hear you and answer you. Remember, flesh is involved, and flesh is often slow to die.

God wants all of you and He wants all of me. Tests provide us with the opportunity to yield more of our vessels unto Him for His exclusive use. Greater assignments require greater purification and sanctification. This is not an easy process. More than once, as Mother Fludd encouraged me to persevere and not give up, I told her I did not want His next assignment for me.

Yet here I am, thrust back into this beautiful haven of rest and peace—on the mend in every way—writing this chapter. Oh, the goodness and mercy of God, the love of my Father, and the love of Jesus for me, His bride.

During an especially dark period of this test, like Job, I felt that God had abandoned me. In fact, as I studied the book of Job, I realized that Job had often felt as I did. This was actually comforting because I had fallen into the enemy's trap of condemnation, guilt, and judgment, even though I knew that Jesus had dealt with all of it for me 2000 years ago. Yes, I knew better, but still I succumbed to the trap. I knew better, yet I left the Cross (my only means of victory) and opened the door to the enemy's torments.

But God, in His infinite mercy and grace, heard my cries—and those of my husband and our many-braided cord of friends—and He is bringing me through to the other side. Praise the Lord!

Entering the Promised Land

I mentioned earlier in this chapter that one of the Old Testament books I recently revisited and studied was Joshua. After Moses died, Joshua was commissioned by God to take over and lead His people across the Jordan River to possess the land that He had given to them.

Now after the death of Moses the servant of the LORD it came to pass, that the LORD spoke unto Joshua the son of Nun, Moses' minister, saying, Moses My servant is dead; now therefore arise, go over this Jordan, you, and all this people, unto the land which I do give to them, even to the Children of Israel. Every place that the sole of your foot shall tread upon, that have I given unto you, as I said unto Moses.

—Joshua 1:1-3

 AFTER OUR OWN PERSONAL SEASON IN THE WILDERNESS, GOD BRINGS US OUT INTO OUR VERSION OF THE PROMISED LAND.

It is of interest that Joshua's ministry began at the bank of the Jordan River, where Jesus would eventually be baptized. And that the name *Joshua* is the Hebrew version of the Greek *Jesus.* God's people had wandered in the wilderness for forty long years. Now it was time for them to go in and possess the land, the inheritance that God had given to them.

Likewise, after our own personal season in the wilderness, when we have successfully completed our test, God brings us out into our version of the Promised Land. This is the victory that Christ, our Husband, won for His brides 2000 years ago.

In verse 3 of chapter 1, we see that God wills His children to be totally free of their former owners or masters. This is exactly what Jesus' finished work at the Cross obtained for us. We no longer need to be bound to any of that which previously enslaved us. The price (penalty) was paid so we can now be free. God wants each one of us to live in total victory over the world, the flesh, and the devil, but we must allow the Holy Spirit to affect this truth in our own lives. He intends for all that impedes our progress with the Lord to be removed. But that requires purification—purging of all that hinders and is not of God—the process of sanctification that involves fiery tests.

I have already mentioned that I felt abandoned by God; then ashamed and condemned for feeling that way, which is the work of Satan. If he cannot deceive you into condemning yourself, he has other instruments—people who will help you condemn yourself!

In the midst of a particularly difficult time, as I studied the Old Testament book of Job, I discovered that Job, who was considered by many to be the greatest man of faith, also felt abandoned by God during his fiery test.

The book of Job, the oldest book of the Bible, is believed to have been written by Moses. It addresses the timeless question of why good people are afflicted. This difficult question was the first such question addressed and answered in the Bible. Fiery tests are for man's sanctification. Remember, God looks at the heart. He sees what we cannot see. He sees potential— people He can prune and prepare for His use. God permitted Satan to afflict Job in order to perfect his character and increase his holiness.

In verse 1 of chapter 1, we read that Job was upright in character and feared God. He was neither sinless nor perfect (none of us are—and will never be), but Job desired to do all he could to please the Lord.

I want to revisit the idea of "sinless perfect." Even as Christ's brides, we will never be sinless perfect. This is why we must keep our eyes fixed on Jesus and the Cross, continually placing our faith in the One Who alone lived the perfect, sinless life and became our Substitute so we could enjoy the victory that He alone won for us. Our righteousness comes no other way than through the finished work of the Son. Yes, even after becoming His bride. Lack of understanding or acceptance of this, will keep us in a cycle of defeat. Remember, even Paul thought he should be able to live a perfect or sinless life once he accepted Christ.

Here is another scripture that is worthy of meditation:

> *For all have sinned, and come short of the Glory of God.*
>
> —Romans 3:23

 WE WILL *NEVER* STOP NEEDING JESUS AND THE CROSS TO EXPERIENCE THE VICTORY OUR HEARTS SO DESIRE.

The original Greek says that all have sinned (*and keep sinning*) and come short (*and keep coming short*) of the Glory of God.

You see, we will NEVER stop needing Jesus and the Cross to experience the victory our hearts so desire— the victory He obtained for us.

Now, back to Job. I encourage you to read or re-read this book, asking the Holy Spirit to unveil truths that will enhance your walk with God. Following are some scriptures that will give you insight about how Job felt during his tests.

The Testing of Job

> *Wherefore is light given to him that is in misery, and life unto the bitter in soul; which long for death, but it comes not; and dig for it more than for hid treasures.*
>
> —Job 3:20-21

Job questioned why the Lord would give life if it was to be filled with such misery, and he longed for death.

> *For the thing which I greatly feared is come upon me, and that which I was afraid of is come unto me.*
>
> —Job 3:25

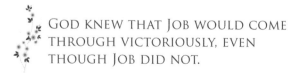

GOD KNEW THAT JOB WOULD COME THROUGH VICTORIOUSLY, EVEN THOUGH JOB DID NOT.

Although many claim that Job's fear brought this horrible test upon him, I do not believe the Bible teaches that. My understanding is that God allowed the hedge of protection around Job to be removed so Satan could afflict him (but *only* to the extent that *God* allowed). This test was for Job's sanctification and our benefit, and for the benefit of all generations. God knew that Job would come through victoriously, even though Job did not.

I also find great comfort in verse 26:

> *I was not in safety, neither had I rest, neither was I quiet; yet trouble came.*
>
> —Job 3:26

"I don't understand this." "I don't like this." "I don't know why this has happened to me." These are all normal reactions to the Job-kind of distress.

I want to briefly discuss Job's three "friends." None of them understood the truth about his test, yet, in the flesh—in their self-righteousness and deception— all three assumed they had all the answers. And they pierced him to the core.

WE CANNOT CONTINUE TO HOLD UNFORGIVENESS IN OUR HEARTS AND EXPECT TO COME THROUGH THE FIRE VICTORIOUSLY.

I am sure that many, if not all of us, have experienced such Job-friends in our own lives—and, sadly, even been a Job-friend ourselves at times! As painful as a Job-friend's supposed revelation and/or assessment of you may be, it is imperative that you forgive him/her as Christ has forgiven you.

We cannot continue to hold unforgiveness in our hearts and expect to come through the fire victoriously. We must forgive those "friends" and then let it go. This is the way of the Cross. Forgive them and *pray* for them. Yes, pray and ask God to bless them, and to bless your relationship with them.

In Job 7:1, we see that Job wanted to die. And because of the extreme pressure of his test, he questioned the purpose of life itself. All he could see, at the moment, was hurt, pain, and destruction. He did not see what had been transpiring in the spirit world—and neither can we. You can see how the book of Job is for our benefit as well.

Have you ever felt as if rest, peace, and sleep eluded you day and night? I certainly have—and so did Job.

> *When I lie down, I say, When shall I arise, and the night be gone? and I am full of tossings to and fro unto the dawning of the day.*
>
> —Job 7:4

He had no rest day or night!

In verse 7, Job further lamented his situation, although his assessment was incorrect. God was patient and longsuffering with him, as He is with you and me. Ultimately, the Lord shows us that no matter how bad the situation may seem, He can change it.

> *Behold, I go forward, but He is not there; and backward, but I cannot perceive Him: on the left hand, where He does work, but I cannot behold Him: He hides Himself on the right hand, that I cannot see Him: but He knows the way that I take: when He has tried me, I shall come forth as gold.*
>
> —Job 23:8-10

IN SPITE OF EVERYTHING, JOB KNEW HIS GOD AND BELIEVED DEEPLY IN HIM.

We all experience times when it seems as if God has left us or hidden Himself from us. Yet in verse 10, Job essentially says that although he cannot sense or perceive God's Presence, God knows exactly what is happening to him, and when the test is over, he "will come forth as gold." In other words, in spite of everything, Job knew his God and believed deeply in Him. Job was confident that in the end—and an end to his troubles was forthcoming—he would come out sanctified and victorious!

Let's look at chapter 30 now. There are 42 chapters in the book of Job, and even in chapter 30, Job was still lamenting his condition.

> *My bones are pierced in me in the night season: and my sinews take no rest. By the great force of my disease is my garment changed: it binds me about as the collar of my coat.*
>
> —Job 30:17-18

Job's physical body was experiencing gnawing, ceaseless pain, and his physical condition seemed to be deteriorating.

In verses 26 and 30, we see that Job thought his situation would change, but it only grew worse. He suffered terrible physical affliction. But through all of it, Job refused to "curse God and die" (Job 2:9), as his wife suggested. Job refused to give up, even though he felt like it at times.

Oh, how this ministered (and ministers) to me.

In the last chapter, we learn that Job prayed for his friends (and the three friends had to seek forgiveness from God), and God ended the test with Job receiving "twice as much as he had before." (See Job 42:7-10.) In verse 12, we learn that the Lord blessed the latter part of Job's life more than the former. It is believed that this test lasted approximately nine to eighteen months.

WE ARE ALWAYS THE ONES WHO NEED TO CHANGE; GOD NEVER NEEDS TO CHANGE.

Now you can understand why the book of Job ministered so deeply to me during my test. The final point from the book of Job that I want to leave with you is this: Job and his three friends had to change—not God! Hmm! We are always the ones who need to change; God never needs to change.

SATAN'S HOLD OVER US WAS BROKEN AT THE CROSS, AND HE HAS NO RIGHT TO HOLD YOU OR ME IN BONDAGE TO ANY SIN.

It isn't easy to trust God when everything around you is shaking and seemingly growing worse. But don't stop seeking Him. Don't stop crying out to Him. Don't stop pouring out your hurting heart to Him. He is there, even when you feel alone. He is there, and if, or when, the flames get too hot, He will bring you out or cool the flames. That is how much He loves you and me. He desires the very best for us, and He won't do anything to hurt us. He has promised to never leave us nor forsake us, and He cannot lie.

Submit yourselves therefore to God. Resist the Devil, and he will flee from you.

—James 4:7

Resist the Devil

During these past months, I have had to live this verse in ways I never have before. It is only as we are submitted to God that we can successfully resist the devil and cause him to flee from us. Why? Because in submitting to God, we submit to the fact that Jesus defeated and conquered Satan totally at the Cross, thereby setting us free from his rule and right to us and our lives.

In Colossians 2:14-15, we are told that Christ's death forever abolished the Law's demands or decrees that were against us. At the Cross, Jesus atoned for all of our sins for all time; thus, guilt, condemnation, and shame have no place in the Bride of Christ. Satan's hold over us was broken at the Cross, and he has no right to hold you or me in bondage to any sin. How often have we consciously or subconsciously allowed guilt to settle in our bodies, making them—in part or in full—pay for the sin that Jesus already paid for? How many times have we allowed Satan to barrage us with constant reminders of sins that God forgave us for long ago, but we have not yet forgiven ourselves? How skillfully and subtly the enemy uses our shortcomings to turn us away from the Cross and the One Who paid for sins that still consume our thoughts and, thus, control our lives?

GOD CANNOT TURN THE *MANURE* OF YOUR LIFE INTO *FERTILIZER* UNLESS YOU ACCEPT HIS FORGIVENESS.

God cannot turn the *manure* of your life into *fertilizer* unless you accept His forgiveness. So when you're tired of believing a lie and struggling to accomplish what only Jesus could accomplish, accept the forgiveness that has been yours for taking all along. Then God can change the manure of your old life into fertilizer that will give you a fresh new life.

As we progress in our walk with God, we have more and more opportunities to submit to God, resist the devil, and watch him flee from us.

All of us fall short, and at one time or another, we are fearful, weak, doubtful, anxious, and worried.

All too often we turn our eyes from the One Who is greater than our problems or situations.

Even David experienced fear, but he knew the solution:

> *What time I am afraid, I will trust in You.*
> —Psalm 56:3

David did not deny the fact that he was afraid; however, he proclaimed his trust in God in the presence of fear. David understood what it was to be overwhelmed too.

> *From the end of the Earth will I cry unto You, when My heart is overwhelmed: lead Me to the rock that is higher than I.*
> —Psalm 61:2

Do not permit the enemy or well-meaning friends to use you against yourself. Turn to the One Who is higher than those who seek to defeat or destroy you. Let Him lift you up and take you through.

My accident was not God's doing. However, God allowed me to go through this because He knew He could turn the *manure* of the horrible experience into *fertilizer*, material that would help to prepare me for a higher and deeper walk with Him—and an assignment I never expected.

To Job-friends, I say: "Do not be so quick to judge." We all get frustrated as to why healing (or whatever we need) has not yet manifested when we so desire it or assume it should be so now (playing God!) And, yes, we may pray and sincerely believe we have heard from God and received a word directly from Him. But sometimes we are deceived into believing that we have the answer when it may be the flesh, wrong doctrine, or lies of the enemy that have surfaced in the supposed revelation.

I think we all need to step back and realize that people who are walking through the fiery trial, especially if they are brides of Christ and soldiers of the Cross, have prayed and cried out to God—perhaps with no answer yet.

It is not because they cannot hear God, but sometimes part of the test—especially as God moves them to higher realms with Him—is in learning to believe Him when He does not answer, when they cannot feel His Presence and feel abandoned! That is a crossroad—a time to decide if they will believe the One Who said He would never leave us or forsake us—or believe the evidence and taunting of the enemy (sometime, via friends) that oppose God's promises.

Also realize that the one enduring the test may have received the answer and not yet shared it with you. No one is perfect. We all are still serving false doctrine, however unintentionally. All of us, at one time or another, doubt or cry out to God, as the father of the demon-possessed son did in Mark 9:14-29, saying, "Lord, I believe; help Thou mine unbelief (v. 24)."

GOD IS A MERCIFUL, LOVING, AND FORGIVING GOD.

God Is Faithful

God is a merciful, loving, and forgiving God. He is not a God who is just waiting for you or me to fall so He can withhold His blessings. He does not delay the fulfillment of His promises to us, His brides, simply because we are struggling with our faith at the moment.

God may never reveal His reasons for allowing certain things in our lives, but we can be sure that He wants what is best for us. Following His plan for our lives is part of growing in faith and being strengthened in our relationship with Him. It involves abandoning ourselves and our lives to Him unconditionally.

GOD ALLOWS US TO BE PULLED ASIDE OR UPROOTED FROM OUR NORMAL LIVES AND ROUTINES.

It is not an easy road, as a dear servant of God from our Bronx ministry team reminds us, but this road is necessary if we are to fulfill the work He has for us to do. That is why God allows us to be pulled aside or uprooted from our normal lives and routines. Often, in needing our attention, God knows we need a time of resting. Oh, how flesh rebels, especially if we have been very active.

That is one reason this test has been so difficult for me. Life as I knew it suddenly stopped. I could no longer walk, run, or trek through life as I had for so long. I even had doctor's orders to begin walking the day after my miracle heart surgery—and to keep on walking. Some of my best prayer times are when I am walking, hiking, trekking, or just pacing around my home.

> THIS EXPERIENCE HAS MADE ME MORE SENSITIVE TO THE DAILY PAIN OF OTHERS WHO SUFFER IN SILENCE EVERY DAY.

You can imagine the impact of life, as I know it, being arrested, especially when my condition seemed to remain stagnant or worsen. The emotional and mental trauma—in part, due to the medication, but also due to increased assaults of the enemy in a magnitude I had never experienced—seemed overwhelming at times. All of a sudden I understood not being able to pray, not being able to read the Word, and not being able to concentrate. Suddenly I understood the need to cry out to friends I trusted to intercede on my behalf.

It was the humbling of Pat before God and man—the vulnerability of Pat before God and man.

This experience has made me more sensitive to the daily pain of others who suffer in silence every day, struggling to get through another day. I have had to depend upon God just to get up and do simple daily tasks, calling upon Him for His strength, asking for mercy, and thanking Him over and over during each day. And He never fails to strengthen me or enable me to do what most people take for granted. And, yes, He made simple requests—and He still does. I have certainly learned more about spiritual warfare, as has my husband.

IT IS AN EXERCISE IN FAITH TO LEARN TO LOOK EXCLUSIVELY AT JESUS CHRIST AND THE CROSS.

The enemy wants us to believe that pain and suffering are our lot in life during these crisis times. He wants us to think that Jesus may deliver someone else's suffering and pain, but not ours. He may even direct his instruments—those in authority, friends, or even yourself—to work in ways that reinforce his deceits and lies. It is tough to believe God above the apparent situation or circumstance. It is an exercise in faith to learn to look exclusively at Jesus Christ and the Cross, where all that has been trying to defeat you has already been defeated and conquered by Jesus 2000 years ago.

When we make the decision to look to Jesus—and to keep looking to Him—even if we fall along the way, He is there wooing us on to the victory He has already won for us. He is wooing us to new heights with Him!

I did not know what to expect in Lake Placid this year, without Nathan and still mending from the accident. But the Peace and Presence of God is truly amazing, and we are so grateful for His mercies, compassions, and faithfulness that are new each morning, according to Lamentations.

> *This I recall to my mind, therefore have I hope. It is of the LORD's mercies that we are not consumed, because His compassions fail not. They are new every morning: great is Your faithfulness.*
> —Lamentations 3:21-23

THE REFLECTING LAKE

I am walking more than I have in the past several months. I'm walking as I did when Dan, Nathan, and I were here last Christmas. What a blessing. What blessings. What gifts. I can't wait for what God has for us these next few days here on Mirror Lake.

CHAPTER 5

OUR HUSBAND'S SACRIFICE

NEARLY ONE YEAR HAS PASSED SINCE Nathan died, and I am finishing my second book. God removed the pain and anguish of Nathan's death and my serious injury, and He also removed the bitterness, unforgiveness, and guilt that I had heaped upon myself for my error in judgment. And gone is the unforgiveness and bitterness I harbored against Nava for lunging forward, causing me to jam both arches on that giant root. Something broke in me, and I returned home to a sweet, loving puppy that I could finally open my heart to, love, and embrace.

I am walking with Nava more than I ever expected, and I love her companionship. I truly praise God for this miracle!

Now I must digress to Christmas on Mirror Lake. It is amazing what God can do when we surrender our hearts—with all our hurts, pains, vows, and plans—to His love, allowing Him to wash away all that has been binding us. How tenderly He ministers to the broken and calloused heart, gently softening the rough edges so He can penetrate the darkness with His liberating light.

These precious verses truly exemplify my journey these past several months.

> *I waited patiently for the LORD; and He inclined unto Me, and heard My cry. He brought Me up also out of an horrible pit, out of the miry clay, and set My feet upon a rock, and established My goings. And He has put a new song in My mouth, even praise unto our God: many shall see it, and fear, and shall trust in the LORD.*
> —Psalm 40:1-3

Notice that the psalmist David acknowledged his patient waiting for the Lord to answer his cry. For all these months of crying out to God and waiting for Him to answer me, I must admit that my waiting was not always done with patience. I felt so alone, and even forsaken, at times, but I did not give up. God has been here with me in the fire all the time, as He wrought to strengthen me. One of G. E. Patterson's sermons blessed me, so I wrote a few statements, amending parts of his message to personally minister to me:

"Don't let what you are going through shake you or make you doubt My love for you."

"I am in the furnace with you."

Hmm. No matter what you or I may be going through, God is right there with us. No matter what is necessary for our deliverance and victory, God engages us, providing the right conditions and circumstances to bring forth the victory and deliverance from the perverse darkness that was achieved by His Son for us 2000 years ago.

Notice in verse 2 of Psalm 40, that God delivers us out of our pits, setting our feet on a rock, out of and above the pit of miry clay. He is the One Who establishes our goings. We cannot extricate ourselves from the pits we've dug or fallen into, and any attempt to do so only buries us deeper in the mire and clay. Our only hope of escape is by trusting in Jesus Who obtained the victory we need.

Even on our best day, we can never merit or be worthy of the healing, deliverance, or miracle that we desire. Jesus obtained it all from the Father Who was satisfied with His sacrifice for us. The Father, our Father, gave the victory to Jesus so He could give it to us. Remember, it was our Father's love that sent His Son to the Cross so we could be saved, healed, delivered, and set free. Oh, what compassion and love He has extended to us.

In verse 3, we read of the new song God places in the mouth (and heart) of the one He has rescued from the pit. Before I arrived at this place, I revisited the Israelites' deliverance from Pharaoh in Exodus 7-14.

"Let My People Go"

God allowed Pharaoh's heart to become hardened and stubborn, and Pharaoh refused to let God's people go. He increased his demands on the Israelites, hoping to break them. This is how I felt as the burning pain increased and the intensity of the trial magnified. But I learned something about God and the Israelites.

SATAN HAS NO RIGHT OR AUTHORITY IN THE LIFE OF A BRIDE OF CHRIST.

In spite of Pharaoh's demands, the Israelites' strength increased—not on their own, but as they relied upon God, trusting Him to ultimately deliver them. He infused His strength into them mentally, emotionally, and physically as their tasks and burdens increased. And the Lord did that for me too.

Pharaoh was a type of Satan. And today the Lord is still saying to Satan and the spirit world, "Let My people go." Satan has no right or authority in the life of a bride of Christ. In fact, he has no right or authority to administrate the curse, in part or in full, in the Believer's life. Yet when things intensify, we often cave in, turning our attention from Jesus and the victory He won for us. We turn away from the Cross and our loving Husband's protective arms, and consume ourselves with the painful circumstances that have not yet changed—or may have worsened.

Of course, the enemy is right there encouraging doom and gloom, trying to reinforce the lie that the work of the Cross wasn't designed for the likes of us. Again, he wants to convince all of us that God has abandoned us. Satan wants us to think that God is disgusted with us—with our whining, complaining, and unbelief—and has turned away from us. Have you ever heard the enemy's taunts? He specializes in nagging, tormenting threats such as, "Look at yourself. You are in worse shape now than when you first believed that message of the Cross. Your 'Husband' has abandoned you." Lies, lies, lies!

Even Abraham, whose faith is mentioned and acclaimed in both the Old and New Testaments, had his moments of weakness, fear, and doubt. We are all but human flesh, and God knows that. That's why He sent His Son to die on the Cross for us. He still loves us, despite what we have done (or what we may do in the future).

We discussed Paul's frustrating and defeating struggles with his flesh after becoming a Believer. He, too, thought he could live a life (in his own efforts) that glorified God. Yet even the greatest of all the apostles repeatedly failed in such efforts. Why? Because they attempted to live that life apart from depending on the Son and the victory He alone had won.

> WE ARE TO LIVE IN TOTAL DEPENDENCE ON WHAT HE OBTAINED FOR US AT THE CROSS.

> *For I delight in the Law of God after the inward man: but I see another Law in my members, warring against the Law of my mind, and bringing me into captivity to the Law of sin which is in my members. O wretched man that I am! Who shall deliver me from the body of this death? I thank God through Jesus Christ our Lord. So then with the mind I myself serve the Law of God; but with the flesh the Law of sin.*
>
> —Romans 7:22-25

Paul so desired to please God. He desperately wanted to live his life free from that which held him bound, yet he saw in his members that which is contrary to God. Even as a bride of Christ, no longer married to the Law, Paul attempted to live for God via self-will and self-effort. We do the same thing today, and we will continue to fail in our efforts until, like Paul, we realize that our lives are in Christ. In other words, we are to live in total dependence on what He obtained for us at the Cross.

This is a day-to-day dependency on what our loving Husband obtained for us, His brides. Even the most consecrated brides will fail if they stop depending, constantly and exclusively, on the finished work of the Son. But the Holy Spirit is always there to teach, guide, and prompt us—ever wooing us back when we fall away. This is the way of victory—the one and only way.

Never Give Up—God Doesn't!

"I thank God through Jesus Christ our Lord" (verse 25). Just knowing the struggles, failings, and weaknesses of Job and Paul helped me through these seemingly endless months. God did not give up on them, and He hasn't given up on me (or you). He saw them through, and He's seeing me through all the way to victory!

Revisiting the Israelite's deliverance from Egypt and the oppression of Pharaoh ministered to me too. The Israelites erroneously thought Pharaoh would obey God's command to let His people go the first time he heard it. Not so! Did God lie to them? No! Their cries were heard and their prayers were answered, but their experience contradicted their present, natural circumstances. Likewise, God heard and answered my cries. However, when the answer didn't come immediately, or after several weeks that became months, Satan began launching his attacks on me. But God allowed all of this to strengthen me and to purge and purify me in preparation for my victory.

It turns out that my injuries healed a while back, and I have been dealing with those *conformation* issues that had been lurking beneath the surface, waiting to erupt. My foot surgeon believes (as do my husband and I) that the injury/accident just advanced the timetable with a vengeance. It was on Mirror Lake that I found the surgeon God had handpicked for me, just as He had done for my miracle seven years ago.

GOD'S PLAN FOR US INCLUDES
WORSHIP, PRAISE, THANKSGIVING, AND
CONFESSION OF THE WORD IN A TIMELY
AND HOLY SPIRIT-INSPIRED WAY.

Did I wonder why it took so long? Of course I did. But I learned some things in this beautiful Olympic haven, far away from the faces of well-meaning friends—some of whom expressed doctrines I had served before the message of the Cross pierced my heart. Pray more, confess more, worship, worship, worship—praise, praise, praise. Such doctrine left me wondering if I had done enough yet. Instead of revering the Father out of love, I feared that He might abandon me if I didn't do enough—or didn't do it perfectly, to His satisfaction. I wondered if God was going to punish me further. Now I know Jesus bore all the punishment I deserve—or ever will deserve.

God's plan for us includes worship, praise, thanksgiving, and confession of the Word in a timely and Holy Spirit-inspired way, but too often, we allow these God-inspired acts to become human works. Ever so subtly, we leave Romans 7:25, and fall into the trap of trying to do enough to finally satisfy God so He will grant the answer to our prayers.

But I learned that such works are unnecessary and futile, because the answer—promised to me because of Jesus' finished work at the Cross—was already granted before I prayed. The Husband's love, compassion, and mercy for His brides have us covered.

Here in this placid atmosphere of God's beauty, I find myself being restored to health and wholeness. The peace and serenity of the lake and surrounding mountains allow me to just be myself before God. I am alone in our suite, yet not really alone. I am very aware of His Presence. I am the bride who arrived five days ago, wounded, hurt, and seemingly beaten. Today I am very different from the woman I was a week ago.

I was amazed at the chastisement I received when I tried to explain to some of my friends about the burning pain I experienced 24-7 for days and weeks on end. "Not enough faith; not enough confessions. Keep suffering, remembering that the Lord suffered for you," they said. Not very encouraging words for a suffering friend!

Doctors could not ascertain why I was experiencing such debilitating pain, even after a myriad of tests. One doctor correctly suspected a conformation issue, but could not prove it because that was not his specialty. Yes, it was warfare, big-time. When you are wracked with pain 24-7 for months on end without sleeping, you can't even pray at times. Yes, I called upon the name of Jesus. And I picked myself up by the bootstraps when reprieves came and I had some strength. But during those very challenging times, our wonderful, *non-judgmental* friends took over, praying and interceding for Dan and me.

Oh, I have learned so much about not being too quick to judge other people. Now, when I see a man or woman, who looks healthy and young, walking slowly or hesitantly, I understand, as never before.

HEALING IS A REVELATION OF WHO GOD IS, NOT OF WHO WE ARE.

Here on Mirror Lake, I continue to reflect and reason together with God. For far too long, I have held a distorted image of Him, often separate from my Husband, God's Son. Now I understand that my Father and Jesus, my Husband, truly are One.

Healing is a revelation of who God is, not of who we are. Our crises, tragedies, and devastations become opportunities for our Father to show His unconditional love and goodness toward us. Only when we have truly *experienced* His love for us can we learn to trust Him, His wisdom, and His goodness in the fiery tests, knowing that we will not have to stay in the test one moment longer than He says.

This whole situation has strengthened my husband, too, making him bolder in his faith, more resolute, and more the "battle-ax" of our family. What a glorious Christmas we had—walking along the lake at a faster pace than before. We were thanking God, resting in His Presence, knowing that I will receive my next set of marching orders when I return home.

Surviving the Tests

I truly thank God for the blessings He bestowed on Dan and me in this peaceful haven. He did a great work in our lives—spirit, soul, and body—fulfilling the desires of our hearts. I was even healed enough to enjoy two dogsled rides around the lake.

WHAT SATAN MEANT FOR EVIL, GOD TRULY HAS TURNED FOR MY GOOD.

I had always wanted to experience a dogsled ride, and this year I did. What a sense of peace, freedom, and exhilaration as the excited team awaited their master's command to go forward. Their utter joy at traversing the lake at an amazing speed captivated us, and we joined them in the excitement. How thrilling it was to glide with ease through the beauty of God's creation—the peaceful lake and sun-kissed, glistening high peaks—under a beautiful blue sky. I felt so free and unburdened as I rested in my husband's arms. I just leaned back into Dan's arms and enjoyed the rides.

Here I am, coming through this test victoriously. What Satan meant for evil, God truly has turned for my good. Of course, I wish I didn't have conformation issues that required surgeries to correct both feet, but this was God's plan for my healing, deliverance, and victory. I must say that, during the past several months, more doctors than I ever expected now have copies of my first book. And all of them are familiar with my miracle heart testimony.

I want to leave you with a greater understanding of Jesus' sacrifice for us, and the ultimate defeat of Satan's authority in the life of a bride of Christ. Satan has absolutely no right to administer the curse—in part or in full—in the lives of Believers. Oh, how blessed we are to have a Husband Who provides protection for us against all the tricks of the enemy!

As I write this, we are preparing to celebrate Resurrection Sunday in a few weeks. What an appropriate time to expound on the love of God for us that resulted in the sacrifice of His only Son and our Husband. God's incredible love for us included a plan for our redemption before the foundation of the world.

DO YOU REALIZE THAT GOD WANTS TO ENJOY FELLOWSHIP WITH YOU?

When man (Adam and Eve in the Garden of Eden) sinned against God, Satan obtained the legal right to administer the curse in man's life. All of us were born under the curse and into the devil's domain. But I remind you that there is only one God, and He permitted all the authority Satan obtained because of man's sin. Man did not and does not incur God's wrath. Sin was and is the culprit.

God's purpose has always been to have fellowship and relationship with man and for man to dwell in and experience His glory. Do you realize that God wants to enjoy fellowship with you?

The Tabernacle

As you probably know, God's chosen people, the Israelites, were His special treasure. God dwelt among His people in the wilderness; He was in their midst— not in their spirits as New Testament children know and experience. He dwelled in a physical tent, specially designed and constructed according to His specifications. This dwelling tent was called the tabernacle.

Let us examine the structure of the tabernacle. First, one entered an open court, which housed a large, brass altar and a brass dish known as a laver. Beyond this courtyard was the actual tent. The holy place was inside the first door. Inside that door was a veil, beyond which was the Holy of Holies.

The outer court was illuminated by natural light, whereas the holy place was lit via a golden candlestick. Inside the Holy of Holies, where God dwelled, His own glory illuminated the room. A box made of acacia wood overlaid with gold was the sole piece of furniture inside the Holy of Holies. The top of this box was composed of pure gold, and the ends were fashioned into cherubim. The lid was the mercy seat, and the box it rested on was called the ark of the covenant.

Most of us are familiar with the Ten Commandments found in the Old Testament book of Exodus 20:3-17. The ark of the covenant contained the two tablets on which were written the Ten Commandments. Malcolm Smith refers to these commandments as "God's statement of love." God's love and holiness truly emanated from the ark of the covenant throughout the encampment, which was twelve miles in diameter.

Although man's sin in the Garden of Eden resulted in his expulsion from God's dwelling place, the place of His glory, God never forsook His people. While His people wandered in the wilderness, God chose to dwell or tent with His people in this tabernacle.

How can this be? Man sinned, and spiritual separation (death) occurred. In himself, man has no hope or ability to keep even one, let alone all, of the Ten Commandments, yet God still chose to dwell with His people in the wilderness. How could this be? Man's sin separated him from God, giving Satan the legal right to administer the curse in man's life. Yet God, who loves you and me, instituted a Law that permitted man to be restored to fellowship with God through the sacrifice of a sinless One on behalf of sinful man.

Obviously, the tabernacle was not physically large enough to accommodate all of God's people, so God instituted the following plan. From the tribe of Levi, Aaron's family was set apart as the priests of God, with Aaron being the first high priest. He represented all of God's people. When Aaron entered the Holy of Holies, he essentially carried all twelve tribes of God's people into the Presence of God with him. So God's people dwelled in the Holy of Holies via Aaron.

Remember, God's people were protected within the twelve-mile diameter of their encampment. Outside this twelve-mile limit, Satan dwelled and administered the curse, but God's people were ensconced in His unconditional and eternal love.

When the high priest entered the Holy of Holies, it was as if each person in that encampment entered with him into the glory of God.

Perhaps you already know the type of Christ this represents. Let us look at the garments the high priest wore. His breastplate was composed of precious stones representing all twelve tribes. Each person could visibly see their own tribe represented on this breastplate. So when the high priest entered the Holy of Holies, he carried them with him, on his heart, into God's compassion and love.

More stones, representing the tribes, were displayed on the shoulders of the high priest's robes. Once again, each person had a visual aid of being carried on his high priest's shoulders into the Holy of Holies, the very Presence of God. For us Believers, brides of Christ, Jesus our High Priest carried us on His shoulders!

When the high priest moved within the tabernacle, he was carrying each person with him. If we had been alive then, it would be likened to each of us watching as our representative high priest carried us into that tabernacle.

The Sacrifice

What happened back then when one sinned? God instituted the Law of substitutionary sacrifice before the foundation of the world. A sinless, guiltless one could die in place of the guilty one—thus, animal sacrifice.

When the appropriate animal was selected, the guilty one would lay his hands upon the animal and confess his sin. The animal was then killed, and its blood was sprinkled upon the ground. Man's sin was then covered. Can you imagine how many times one would have to do this in the course of a year? For that reason, God decreed there would be one day per year when He would receive all of the individual sin offerings into one offering that would finish the sin offering requirement for the year. In this case, the blood of the animal was carried by the high priest into the Holy of Holies and sprinkled upon the mercy seat for that one time each year. This day is known as the Day of Atonement (Yom Kippur). When the blood of the animal was sprinkled on the mercy seat, God was satisfied and the sins of all the people were covered by this blood.

The blood of an animal, no matter how unblemished, could only *cover* sin. It had no capacity to wash sin away. But during this time, such animal sacrifice was the only means of approach into the Presence of God. Think about this—the high priest carrying the blood, on behalf of every one of God's people, into the Holy of Holies.

Furthermore, on this Day of Atonement, the high priest exchanged his beautiful robe, with precious stones that set him apart from the people, for the robe or garment of a regular priest. This was a white, linen robe or garment. Thus, there was no distinction between him and another priest. He was like any ordinary man. Hmmm.

On this special day, two goats were required for sacrifice instead of the usual one. On this day, all the Israelites gathered together, knowing that all the sins they had committed for that year were about to be covered. All of their sins were dealt with at once on this day.

Lots were cast to determine each goat's role. The first goat selected was designated for Yahweh, the name of Covenant God—the Lord. The remaining goat was for Azazel. The high priest (*your* personal representative before God, if you lived during that time) laid both hands upon the goat "for Yahweh." The actual Hebrew translation says that he pushed his hands onto that goat, thereby leaning all the weight of all the sins onto that goat. The whole weight of all the sins committed by each individual was pushed onto that goat. Can you imagine what it would have been like to wait for this one day when you could relinquish all the weight of all your sins from the year? How liberating! How freeing!

At this point, the high priest confessed the sins of all the people over this goat. If you had been there, you would have heard your own sins being confessed by your substitute high priest, recognizing that by this very act your sins were being removed from you.

Also you would face the harsh reality of an innocent goat bearing the guilt, shame, and filth of your sins, ultimately bearing the death penalty that you deserved.

After the high priest completed the confession of the people's sins, he cut the goat's jugular vein. At last, the blood was shed—and with this shedding of blood came the covering of the people's sins. That innocent goat died in their place, paying the penalty for all their sins for the entire year.

On this Day of Atonement, the goat's blood was collected in a basin—instead of dropping to the earth—and taken by the high priest into the Holy of Holies. Remember, only the high priest could enter the Holy of Holies, and only once a year. If you and I had been there, we would have been waiting while the high priest entered the Holy of Holies to sprinkle the goat's blood on the mercy seat on our behalf. Can you imagine the suspense as the high priest disappeared into the Holy of Holies and could no longer be seen? All awaited his return, for this would signify that for the rest of this year, the people would live in God's Presence. The blood of the goat designated for Yahweh was accepted by the Lord as a covering for the people's sins for that year. So God's glory filled the twelve-mile encampment of His people—a light in the dark world outside that camp.

Every year, such a sacrifice was required to satisfy the sin-debt of the people. Again, the blood of the goat only *covered* the sins of the people; it never washed sin away. So the return of the high priest to the people signified another year in the Presence and glory of God. But what about the second goat, the one designated for Azazel?

It is believed that Azazel was another name for the devil. The high priest placed his hands on that goat and confessed the sins of the people. Why would he do this when the blood of the first goat covered the people's sins? Well, a rope was placed around this goat's neck, and a special messenger was chosen to lead this goat for Azazel into the wilderness.

This truly was a visual aid of the sins that had been covered by the blood of the goat selected for Yahweh and accepted by Him. Thus, all the sins that had been covered by the blood were now were being carried away into the wilderness…

> *As far as the east is from the west, so far has he removed our transgressions from us.*
> —Psalm 103:12

Remember, the people witnessed the shed blood of Yahweh's goat, but they did not see it being sprinkled or accepted. With the goat for Azazel, the people actually saw their sin (which had been paid for) being carried into the wilderness. This goat was led outside that twelve-mile radius to the realm of darkness, where Satan had legal rights over sinners—where he could legally execute or administer the curse. So the goat for Azazel showed that the sins of God's people were covered and were not in Satan's domain. The blood of God's ordained sacrifice was accepted. Wow! What a type of Christ. What a type of what Christ, our Husband, did for us, his brides.

This is truly a message to the devil that God's people are no longer under Satan's authority. This was—and is—a message observed in the seen realm of what transpired in the unseen spiritual realm. Wow! This is truly the victory of God's plan of redemption as witnessed by man and Satan and his kingdom. Remember, Satan had no power over man—any man—until man sinned, but with God's acceptance of the shed blood, Satan's power over man ended. What a type of Christ! What a foretaste of the ultimate once-and-forever sacrifice of God's beloved Son.

The Ultimate and Final Sacrifice

In God's appointed time, Jesus, the ultimate and final sacrifice, came and "offered Himself without spot to God" (Hebrews 9:14), forever ending the need for further sacrifice.

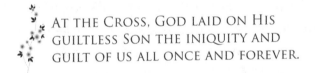

AT THE CROSS, GOD LAID ON HIS
GUILTLESS SON THE INIQUITY AND
GUILT OF US ALL ONCE AND FOREVER.

Jesus truly was the one and only sinless Man—the One who could take the place of all man before God, on our behalf. Jesus is the ultimate tabernacle in whom there is room for all of God's people. No longer do we wait outside the Holy of Holies. We Believers are invited in to dwell in God's Presence forever.

At the Cross, God laid on His guiltless Son the iniquity and guilt of us all once and forever. His finished work on the Cross bought us back from Satan's realm so we could enjoy daily fellowship with our Father.

Then on the third day, Jesus rose from the dead (as did Believers, positionally) to newness of life, freed from the bondage and chains of Satan and the sin nature (see Romans 6). And by His ultimate sacrifice, Jesus, our Husband, has carried us, his brides, into the Presence of God where we can dwell forever. In the resurrection, we (positionally) rose with Him to the newness of life where we now stand.

Think about this. Jesus, the final High Priest (our High Priest and Husband), who is, Himself, the final Sacrifice, brings His own Blood before God on our behalf, becoming the final mercy seat and the seat of God's final satisfaction.

In the Old Testament tabernacle, there was no chair in the Holy of Holies because no priest could sit down. Why? Because until Jesus, the Final Sacrifice, the work/plan of salvation was not finished. But when Jesus ascended to heaven, He sat down at the right hand of the Father because it was all done. Not only were man's sins covered, but they were washed away—cleansed by that precious atoning Blood of the spotless Lamb of God.

No more sacrifices would be necessary because this sacrifice had covered and cleansed all sin for all time. Oh, what rest and peace we have when we realize the truth of this. There is nothing left to do. All has been accomplished by Jesus at the Cross. Our Father beckons us to come and rest and abide in this finished work of His Son.

 SATAN MAY TRY TO HURL GUILT, SHAME, AND CONDEMNATION AT US, BUT FOR BELIEVERS, ALL OF THAT HAS BEEN WASHED AWAY.

Jesus' death, burial, and resurrection testified to the whole world and the kingdom of darkness that Satan's right of authority over all who believe in Jesus Christ had ended. Satan has no more say because Jesus' own shed Blood on the mercy seat declares that Believers are justified and righteous, standing before the Father as if they were Jesus. Satan may try to hurl guilt, shame, and condemnation at us, but for Believers, all of that has been washed away. Jesus and the Father resolved the sin problem for us once and for all, and Satan could do nothing to stop it. He had no say then, and he has no say now.

This gives new meaning to Revelation 12:11:

And they overcame him by the blood of the Lamb, and by the word of their testimony; and they loved not their lives unto the death.

Our power in overcoming Satan and his kingdom is in resting and trusting in the Blood sacrifice of Jesus and through faith in His finished work.

Buried with Him in Baptism, wherein also you are risen with Him through the Faith of the operation of God, Who has raised Him from the dead. And you, being dead in your sins and the uncircumcision of your flesh, has He quickened together with Him, having forgiven you all trespasses; blotting out the handwriting of Ordinances that was against us, which was contrary to us, and took it out of the way, nailing it to His Cross; and having

*spoiled principalities and powers, He made a show
of them openly, triumphing over them in it.*
                                        —Colossians 2:12-15

We (positionally) died with Jesus, were buried with Him, and rose from the dead with Him (Romans 6:3-5). Herein lies our victory. Satan and all of his cohorts were defeated at the Cross. Some of us have been waging war against an already defeated enemy! With all sin atoned for by the Blood of Christ, once and for all, Satan's legal hold over man ended for all time. Remember, it was sin that initially gave Satan that legal right, but Jesus, the perfect sacrifice, rescinded that right.

Thus, referring back to Revelation 12:11, we place our faith in the eternal Blood of Jesus (on that mercy seat in the Holy of Holies) that says "all done." There is nothing, no-thing, left to pay for!

Our power is in the Holy Spirit who administers the reality of the authority and power in the Blood as well as the whole of the finished work of the cross. Thus, our position in "pleading the Blood" should be one of boldly referring to the authority of that Blood.

If all has been settled at the Cross, then this should be our position regarding "pleading the Blood."

This year has been a very difficult year for Dan and me. It has been filled with death, grief, sorrow, injury, and intense and seemingly relentless pain. I have known times of feeling abandoned by God (wilderness times) and times when His strong Presence, glory, and even His aroma filled my place. I know what it is like to want to give up—and, like Job, I sometimes wonder why God kept me alive. Yet here I am, finished with this book—and just days after the death of a wonderful, dear friend.

I have learned a lot about spiritual warfare these past months. My husband and I had a multitude of opportunities to give up and quit, but because of our abiding faith in God and wonderful caring friends who helped sustain us, we decided to follow God's script for our lives.

Spiritual warfare really involves fighting a war that has already been won. Our enemy, Satan, and his kingdom are already defeated foes. Yet many Believers wage war as if this were not so, fighting an enemy they erroneously believe still has some authority in their lives. Sometimes their actions are so subtle that they don't realize they are doing this. I know because I did that. Like many other people, I was erroneously taught to do that. But these past several months have certainly taught me otherwise. Yes, there is a very real battle, but most often it is in our minds. Sometimes the enemy hurls such strong attacks (mental, emotional, and physical) that it appears to be a war. But God says the battle was won—totally won—2000 years ago. So don't succumb to the temptation to arm yourself for a fight with an enemy that has already been defeated.

Ephesians 6 discusses our spiritual battle. It is described as a wrestling match in which we are instructed to stand, and having done all, to keep standing (Ephesians 6:13). How can one successfully wrestle while standing? In the Greek, the word for *stand* means "hold your own." In other words, stand for what is already yours. You do not fight for that which is already yours—you hold on to it. Yes, I know what it is to fight and stand there (in the place of victory, the positional place of the covenant promises I have with God), saying, "I have what God says is mine."

OUR HUSBAND'S SACRIFICE

OUR FAITH IS PLANTED, AND AS WE STAND AND HOLD ON TO THE BLOOD SACRIFICE AT THE CROSS, THE HOLY SPIRIT IS FREE TO ADMINISTER THESE TRUTHS TO OUR LIVES.

God is who He says He is to me, and He is doing for me now what He said He would do. Jesus' Blood and the stripes on His back are enough for me because they have done—and are doing—exactly what God said they would do.

So as I take my position in Christ, as His bride, the Holy Spirit can affect these truths in my life. This is how we overcome. Our faith is planted, and as we stand and hold on to the Blood sacrifice and the Son's finished work at the Cross, the Holy Spirit is free to administer these truths to our lives. This is how those battles in and for our minds are won. And each one of us must personally learn this way of victory. Our loving Father designs and permits circumstances in our lives to purify us and draw us closer to Him. And as our relationship with Him deepens, we gain a new appreciation for His unconditional love that bought our freedom through His finished work at the Cross.

It has been a long and often difficult journey this past year, but God has brought us through. Now I am ready for the script He has for me next. I'm ready for His complete healing and restoring Rx for my feet. So I go on, knowing it is so. Why? Because He said so. I have my Father's Word on it!

Through all of the grief, sorrow, and intense pain, my loving Husband has been carrying me all the way to victory—the victory He won all those years ago. AMEN.

I pray that you, too, will gain a greater understanding of the love of the Father and His Son—the ultimate love of the Husband for His brides. Whatever circumstances you have faced—or are now facing—He is your answer. I encourage you to surrender yourself as never before into the strong, loving arms of your Husband. It is a wonderful place of peace and security. AMEN.

Prayer for a Personal Relationship with the Lord Jesus Christ

Od loves you, no matter who you are or what you have done. You are not here by accident. God sent "His only Begotten Son [so] that whosoever believes in Him should not perish, but have Everlasting Life" (John 3:16).

> *For by Grace are you saved through Faith; and that not of yourselves: it is the Gift of God: Not of works, lest any man should boast.*
>
> —Ephesians 2:8-9

We can do nothing to earn salvation. It is a gift from God to anyone who will receive.

If you would like to give your heart and life to Jesus Christ, you can do so right now. Simply pray the following prayer with a sincere heart:

Dear God in Heaven, I come to You, acknowledging that I am a sinner. I realize my need for a Savior, and I ask You now to save me (my soul) and cleanse me from all my sins. I acknowledge Jesus Christ, Who purchased a full redemption for me by His finished work at Calvary. I call upon Jesus Christ to be my Savior and Lord because I believe Jesus died and rose for me. Thank You. I am now saved. Amen.

REFERENCES

The following resources helped me with my research for this manuscript.

Lloyd-Jones, D.Martyn, *Romans—Exposition of Chapter 7:1-8:4, The Law, Its Functions and Limits,* ©1973, Zondervan Publishing House, Grand Rapids, MI.

Smith, Malcolm, *Living Without Guilt,* three-hour audio cassette teaching, distributed by Unconditional Love International, P.O. Box 1599, Bandera, TX 78003.

Patterson, Gilbert Earl, presiding bishop of the Church of God in Christ, the nation's largest African-American Pentecostal denomination until his passing in March 2007. Also pastor of Temple of Deliverance Church of God in Christ, Memphis, TN and founder of

Bountiful Blessings Ministries (BBM), which is viewed internationally on Black Entertainment Television and the Trinity Broadcasting Network weekly, as well as on local television stations throughout the nation.

Swaggart, Jimmy, *The Expositor's Study Bible, King James Version,* July 2005, Jimmy Swaggart Ministries, Baton Rouge, Louisiana.

Vine, W.E., *Vine's Expository Dictionary of Old and New Testament Words*, July 1997, Nelson Reference, Thomas Nelson Publishers, Nashville, Tennessee.

ABOUT THE AUTHOR

P AT NOLAN IS AN ORDAINED MINISTER of the Gospel and teaches and ministers worldwide, often appearing as a guest on Christian television. She has a graduate degree in Biometry and Statistics from Cornell University, and before accepting the call to ministry, she taught Statistics at Ithaca College in Ithaca, New York. Her ministry was radically changed by the message of the Cross, and she teaches seminars that unveil the Father's love as shown through Jesus Christ and His finished work at the Cross. Pat and her husband Dan, a renowned physicist, reside in upstate New York.